A Graceful Waiting

A Graceful Waiting

When There's Nothing More that You Can Do,
God's Deepest Work Has Just Begun

Jan Frank

SERVANT PUBLICATIONS
ANN ARBOR, MICHIGAN

Vine Books is an imprint of Servant Publications especially designed to serve evangelical Christians.

Scriptures verses marked NASB are from the New American Standard Bible, © the Lockman Foundation 1960, 1962, 1963, 1968, 1971, 1972, 1973, 1975, 1977. Scripture verses marked NKJV are from The New King James Version, © 1979, 1980, 1982, Thomas Nelson, Inc., Publishers. Scripture quotations marked NIV are taken from the HOLY BIBLE, NEW INTERNATIONAL VERSION®, © 1973, 1978, 1984 by International Bible Society. Used by permission of Zondervan Publishing House. All rights reserved. Scripture verses marked LB are taken from *The Living Bible*, © 1971, owned by assignment by KNT Charitable Trust. All rights reserved.

Lyrics to "A Heart That Knows You," by Twila Paris, (© 1992) used by permission of Ariose Music.

Published by Servant Publications
P.O. Box 8617
Ann Arbor, Michigan 48107

Cover design: Michael Andaloro

96 97 98 99 00 10 9 8 7 6 5 4 3 2 1

Printed in the United States of America
ISBN 0-89283-967-8

Dedication

To my maternal grandmother,
Rosie Nell Garrett
(1893-1978),
and
my paternal grandfather,
Raymond Roy Mitchell
(1908-1974),
whose prayers and godly wisdom
blessed my life.
I can't wait to see you in glory!

Contents

Acknowledgments

I could not have written this book without the committed, fervent prayers of many faithful friends. I was encouraged many times by those who dropped me a note, called to ask how the book was coming, or faxed a communiqué of Scriptures or prayers that were offered in my behalf. To the many men and women across the country who interceded for me, I offer a most grateful thanks. I know your prayers sustained me many times when the task at hand seemed insurmountable.

I want to give special thanks to my friend, Dr. Daniel Fleeman, and his Thursday night men's group in Wichita, Kansas. Your faithful prayers and faxes over these months lifted my spirits, brought a smile to my face, and blessed me more than you know.

With deep gratitude, thanks very much to:

My friend, Marian McFadden, whose love for the Word of God and commitment to the integrity of the Scriptures continually inspires and challenges me. You are a special friend who often reminds me of truths I've spoken, but neglected to live out. Thanks for your continued encouragement, intercession, and friendship!

Ginny and Patsy, my dearest friends, who believe in me

and calm my fears through tender words by telephone—even at midnight.

My friends and faithful intercessors: Greg and Susie Kazanjian in Cincinnati; Dotty Stephenson, and Pam Houston.

Lauren Briggs, whose friendship has blessed my life and whose computer skills, along with those of Dave Morris, have rescued me countless times.

Jenni Key, whose valuable insights and spiritual depth I greatly admire.

Friends like Mae, Jenny, Don, and Mary, and all in our Sunday School class, who prayed for me as I waited and worked through this book on waiting.

Karen Garland, whose prayer vision sustained me during my frantic moments.

Heidi Hess, Diane Bareis, Lonnie Collins Pratt, Kathy Deering, and all those at Servant Publications, whose expertise and vision contributed to this book.

Bert Ghezzi, who believed I had something to say, even when I wasn't so sure I did.

Liz Heaney, my editor, to whom I feel greatly indebted. God sent you to me to help me grow up as a writer. Your keen sense of focus, candid feedback, and expertise have been invaluable to me. I hope this is just the beginning of a lasting friendship!

My precious husband, Don, whose continual encouragement, support, and prayer keep me going from day to day. You have taught me more about loving our Lord than you will ever know. You are God's precious gift to me!

My daughters, Heather and Kellie, whom God uses continually to teach me eternal truths. Thanks for praying, doing extra chores, and loving me when I'm under pressure.

Many who shared their waiting seasons with me. Your insights, personal stories, and perspective contributed to me personally and added depth and meaning to this book.

My "Abba Father," who waits that he might be gracious to me.

I've Been Waiting So Long!

"It was so hard watching her cry. I didn't know what to say," Sunny said. "She's waited so long." I was getting my hair cut as I overheard my hairdresser's assistant, Sunny, talk about her visit to the hospital that morning. Her dear friend, who's been infertile for twelve years, had just gone through a tubal dye study in which dye was injected into her fallopian tubes to determine if there was any obstruction. She was told her tubes were irreparably blocked and that pregnancy was impossible through natural means.

As I listened I was reminded of my sister-in-law, Barb, who month after month made a 45-minute drive to the hospital where she would undergo artificial insemination. Barb told me how she would drive back to the school where she counseled, and in the seclusion of her vice-principal's office lean her head against the wall and cry. She found herself questioning, and often stating her case before God. *I'm not a bad person. Why aren't you letting me have a baby? Is this punishment for something I've done? Please, God, I don't understand.*

After waiting three years, Barb and her husband, Russ, decided to try to adopt. They adopted a little boy they named Brady, and within a month, Barb found out she was pregnant. They now have two precious sons, ten months apart. Barb is convinced this was all a part of God's plan.

Can you relate to these women? Have you ever had to wait for something you longed for? Have you ever:

- Prayed for a wayward child to come back to God?

- Asked God to send you Mr. or Miss Right?

- Waited for your spouse to become more responsive and loving?

- Worked extra hard and waited for a well-deserved job promotion?

- Begged for God to heal someone you love from a terminal illness?

If so, you know how difficult it is to wait.

All of us have at some time in our lives waited for something that we felt embodied our happiness or contentment. We hope, pray, daydream, strive after, and anticipate. For some of us, this is an excruciatingly painful process. Others weather waiting more gracefully. I find myself rather resistant and creative in my attempts to circumvent the waiting. I have been anything but graceful, while God has been abundantly "full of grace."

Over the past few years the Lord has taught me much about waiting. I must confess I was ill-prepared and ill-mannered when waiting came calling at my door.

Entering a Waiting Season

The Saturday before school was to start, my seven-year-old daughter Kellie and I drove by the school to look at the class rosters that were posted on the windows of the office. Several parents and children were already there when we arrived, and Kellie and I stood behind the crowd until we could edge our way through to the front. I scanned the list of the classroom in which we had assumed Kellie would be, but couldn't find Kellie's name. Puzzled, I began scanning other second-grade rosters until I found it. Kellie started to cry.

Trying not to show too much disappointment, I said, "Honey, I'm not sure how that happened, but it's going to be all right. I know you're disappointed. I am, too, but I'm sure things will work out."

Later that evening, my husband Don and I discussed the situation. We agreed that I would write the principal, requesting a classroom change. All would be taken care of in the next week or two. I typed a letter that evening and dropped it off at the school office the next morning.

We did not tell Kellie we were attempting to have her moved. We thought it best that she learn to adapt, even though we were counting on her being moved. But Kellie came home every day upset and disappointed. We had talked for three years about her being in *that other* particular classroom with a teacher she knew already because she had taught her older sister Heather. Most of Kellie's friends were in that teacher's room, and Kellie was having a hard time adjusting.

By the second week of school, I had not received a response from the principal, so I phoned the office and was told no class changes were being considered during the first two weeks of school. I decided to wait until the following week to phone again.

You Just Don't Understand

One afternoon during the third week, I knew something was wrong the minute I picked up the girls after school. Kellie was visibly upset as I asked about her day.

"Mommy, I got in trouble today," she said, as tears dripped down her cheeks.

"What happened, sweetheart?" I asked.

"I was doing my math and the girl next to me asked me a question, so I answered her. The teacher saw me talking and told me I should be working and not talking. She told me I lost points for the day."

"Honey, I'm sorry that happened. Did you try to explain to your teacher that you were answering a question about math?"

"No, she just said I had to lose points."

This experience was particularly hard for Kellie, who had always been a model student. I knew there was probably more to the story, but I suggested she talk to her teacher about what had happened when she went back to school the next day.

The following day Kellie got into the car again, and burst into tears.

"Honey, what's wrong?" I asked.

"Mommy, today I had to sit on a bench and lose my recess."

"How come, sweetie?"

"I don't know. Mommy, the girl who sits next to me doesn't understand the work and she keeps asking me questions. When I was in Mr. Miller's class last year, he liked me to be a good helper."

"Oh, honey, I'm sorry this is happening. Maybe I need to talk to your teacher. That's the first time you ever had to lose a recess, isn't it?"

Kellie was sobbing. I cradled my little girl in my arms and said, "Honey, you're a good girl. Mommy is going to take care of you. I am so sorry this happened." I knew my feelings were far more intense than the situation warranted, but didn't understand why.

I knew Kellie was humiliated. Over the next two days Kellie started exhibiting fears about going to school. She would wake up saying she had a tummyache and didn't think she could go. While I realized that the teacher was not intending to cause my daughter suffering, all I could focus on was my little girl's obvious stress and discomfort. I was afraid of how this situation might affect her attitude toward school, but most of all I was concerned that she feel I was oblivious to her feelings or that I allowed her to remain in a situation that seemed harmful to her. The more I thought about it, the more upset I became. I just had to do something to show my daughter I cared about her pain. I phoned the principal's office that afternoon and made an appointment.

As I talked with the principal the next day, my stomach churned. I calmly explained my concerns for my child. Kellie was brought in and articulated the events of the past few days. I assured the principal that I was not criticizing the teacher, and that my concern was for my daughter's well-being. Kellie was only a child, unable to discern that her difficulties might simply be due to personality differences. I told the principal that Don and I felt it to be in Kellie's best interest to have her moved to another class and the reasons why. I concluded by saying that I'd be happy to meet with the teacher so that there were no ill feelings.

The principal listened intently, but said she was not able to accommodate my request at this time because the other teacher's class was already full. I did not recognize at the time that the principal was merely trying to follow procedural guidelines and look out for the welfare of all involved. All I could see was my hurting child. At the time, I didn't realize my intense reaction was connected to the sexual abuse in my background: My mother had not protected me, and the thought of me not protecting my daughter was unbearable.

Irritated, I replied, "I don't think that you understand. I am not only requesting this as a parent, I'm a licensed Marriage, Family, and Child Counselor, and I see evidence in Kellie's emotional life that indicates this situation is harmful to her. This is not a matter of preference, this has to do with the wellbeing of my child. I would like her changed immediately."

The principal offered her apologies, but refused to grant my request.

I exited the office angrily. *How dare she not respond to my request?* I thought. *Well, she's got another thing coming. I'll picket the school. Better yet, I'm calling the superintendent and then the school board. If Kellie isn't moved, I'll put her in another school. Wait until Don hears about this. I can't believe this is happening. She even knows my husband is a teacher. Why won't she cooperate? Just wait. They don't know who they're dealing with. This is my daughter, and I'm going to see that she's protected!*

Little Did I Know...

Little did I know the significance of this event. God used this situation to catapult me into a season of waiting. He had scripted the notes but failed to ask for my approval.

I often write my prayers in a journal. Before any of this happened I had made a journal entry which expressed my heart's desire. I had no idea that God's answer would be "Wait." I wrote:

Lord, you have challenged me to look within myself. Faith is not faith if we can touch the outcome. Faith operates in absence of outcome. Lord, I want to be a woman of faith—one who believes you in the midst of the confusion when all appears lacking in sense and logic. I do not have that kind of faith. I stepped out once, but I was wrong. Am I holding back from you for fear of another humiliation? I know your goodness and your desire for me—help me to hurdle these obstacles and totally abandon myself to your plan. "So then faith comes by hearing, and hearing by the Word of God" [Romans 10:17, NKJV]. My faith has seemed to waver, Lord, and I feel as though I have disappointed you. Have I allowed seeds of unbelief to destroy my foundations of faith? Or have the foundations had these termites or cracks forever, and they are now just being exposed to the light? Help me to know and to walk and live again by faith that stands against the odds—faith that sees beyond logic and hope—faith that goes beyond my understanding or the tangible outcome. Oh Lord, help me to be a woman of faith!

God used this troublesome situation to teach me about myself and my reactions to the "W" word—"wait." He showed me that godly waiting moves from focusing on *external* circumstances to focusing on what God is doing *internally,* and finally to an *eternal* perspective.

My prayer for you as you read this book is that you will find hope and encouragement. More importantly, I pray you will come to discover, as I did, how God's loving nature is manifested through the waiting seasons of our lives. God himself waits. In the book of Isaiah we are given a wonderful promise in.

Therefore the Lord longs to be gracious to you, and therefore He waits on high to have compassion on you. For the Lord is a God of justice; How blessed are all those who long for Him.   ISAIAH 30:18, NASB

Perhaps you are in a season of waiting. You can't understand why God has not answered your pleas.… You wonder what God is doing. Come with me to the field of my heart where God taught me about what it means to wait on him. The Gardener is waiting there. He's been expecting you.

PART ONE

God's Threshing Floor

TWO

When Waiting Brings Wondering

I couldn't believe Kellie's principal was insisting on following policy. *Didn't she see that my child was hurting? Didn't she care? Why was she resisting my request?* I found myself flipping back and forth between bewilderment and anger. *Why is this happening? How dare she exercise control over my child? What do I do now? She's got another thing coming if she thinks this is over!*

At the time, I had no inkling that God had another agenda. He had my course work all planned out. He declared my major for the next five years and enrolled me in Waiting #101 before I had a chance to review the curriculum. I never wanted to audit such a class, let alone have it as my major!

Waiting 101

When the Lord seemed to be prompting me to write about waiting, I argued, "But Lord, I'm terrible at waiting. You have the wrong person!" The more I thought about it the more I disqualified myself. Every memory I ever had of being impatient, frustrated, argumentative with God about his silences or delays flashed before my mind, supporting my contention of ineligibility. What could I write about? How could *I* tell people about waiting when I spent so much time trying to avoid it?

I was talking about my dilemma over lunch with a friend one day. When I told him I felt so inadequate to write on waiting, he asked me a simple question, "Jan, what do you think 'godly waiting' looks like?"

I paused for a moment and then said, "I picture someone sitting serenely in an oversized chair with a contented face that says, 'all is well.'"

He looked at me seriously, then smiled and said, "Jan, I don't think that is a picture of godly waiting. I think that's denial!"

The more I thought about our conversation, the more I knew he was right. Was my picture of "godly waiting" an unrealistic ideal? Who did I know that I considered to be a "godly waiter"? What did I admire about such people? What did the Scripture have to say about those who wait? Is there a list of traits we should have? Is there a prescription to follow on how to be a successful "waiter"? Who, in the Bible, exemplified "godly waiting"?

For Our God and His Glory

As I read through familiar biblical accounts of waiting, I continually came to the conclusion that God calls us to wait for two primary reasons: for our good and his glory. Consider—

- Abraham, who waited for the fulfillment of the promise of a son,

- Moses, who delivered the nation Israel from the bondage of Egypt,

- Joseph, who trusted God in unjust circumstances and ultimately saved his family from famine,

- Ruth, who through tragedy came to be redeemed by Boaz,

- Hannah, who waited for a son and then gave him back to the Lord, and

- Lazarus, who died and was raised from the dead.

Each was called to a period of waiting. All were witnesses and beneficiaries of the grace and glory of God.

If you are, right now, in a season of waiting and not sure how you got there, you *can* be sure that God has your good in mind. You can be sure because of the record of God's dealings with his people in Scripture. The writer of the letter to the Romans sums it up: "For everything that was written in the past was written to teach us, so that through endurance and the encouragement of the Scriptures we might have hope" (Romans 15:4, NIV).

You may not know how long this season will last or what the final outcome will be. That is what makes it so difficult. Waiting is a process, and there is a process within the process of waiting. But God is faithful in his plans to provide a "future and a hope." This diagram may help to illustrate the waiting process:

These concentric circles represent the three stages of waiting.

The outer stage is the one where our focus is primarily on the externals. We're waiting for God to do something, change something, or bring something to pass. As we proceed

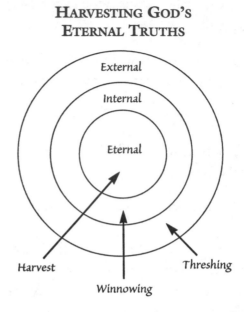

HARVESTING GOD'S ETERNAL TRUTHS

through this stage, we wonder, wander, whine, and even wallow; God is "threshing" us like wheat. He's removing "chaff" from us, unwanted elements that interfere with our usefulness and purity.

The middle stage is an internal, deep cleansing of the heart which can be compared to the winnowing of grain. The evening breezes remove additional impurities from the grain that, if left undetected, could cause harm to those who consume the wheat later. As we wait through this internal stage of weeping, wrestling, and becoming willing, we are being purified and prepared for service by the gentle breezes of God's Spirit at work within our lives.

The inner circle represents the useful harvest—grain which is ready to be ground into flour and baked into bread. In this stage, we become partakers and participants in God's sovereign work. Our focus shifts from the external and internal to the eternal purposes and truths of God. We view life's circumstances more from an eternal perspective. We are less bent on wresting circumstantial change from God and more likely to pursue our relationship with him regardless of our circumstances. Our waiting yields wisdom, wellsprings of joy, and worship for our God.

God uses waiting as his modern day threshing instrument, to help us grow and mature. He takes us to the threshing floor of life's hard circumstances. There we must wait. It is there he executes a deeper work within us, for our good and his glory.

God's Threshing Floor

In America, most of us don't have much contact with the processes necessary to make harvested grain edible. We stop at the store and buy some bread or some flour. On the bag, we might notice an illustration of some wheat stalks, but we take the whole process for granted.

Threshing, especially as practiced in Bible times, is almost unknown to us. What does it entail?

The ancient process of harvesting grain started with reapers who cut the stalks of grain and gathered them into bundles called sheaves. The sheaves were left out to dry. The dried stalks were taken to the threshing floor where the grain kernels were separated by one of several different means. Often, animals such as oxen were used to trample the grain from the chaff. Sometimes, people used a threshing sledge, which was a flat board with metal fragments on the bottom which was dragged over the grain to separate it.[1] It took several days to complete the threshing.

The threshing floor was a circular, flat area of land, "about fifty to a hundred feet in diameter, in the open air, on elevated ground, and made smooth, hardy, and clean." Threshing floors were often elevated pieces of land outside the city where the night winds could more easily blow away the chaff.[2]

After the threshing process removed the grains from the stalks, the mixture remained on the threshing-floor for the winnowing process. In the morning and evening, the breezes would blow more strongly. The farmer would take a winnowing fork with broad prongs, pick up a pile of chaff and grain, and toss it into the air. The heavy grains fell directly to the floor, while the chaff was blown away into another pile away from the good grain.

In some areas the winnowed grain was sifted through a sieve to remove any remaining unwanted matter. The sifted grain was poured into pottery jars and stored, later to be turned into flour for baking to nourish the family and community.[3]

While enduring a season of waiting myself, I began to understand the connection between these ancient agricultural processes of threshing and winnowing and the internal threshing, winnowing, sifting, and pouring out going on in my inner life.

All grain which was harvested had to go to the threshing floor in order to be useful for its intended purpose, which was to provide life and nourishment to God's people. The chaff in our lives, which has no life-giving value, must be separated from the good, life-sustaining "grain."

The waiting season in your life has a purpose. It has been initiated by the loving hand of God to produce in and through your life a greater, more abundant harvest. You may not see it now, but 2 Corinthians 9:10 tells us we will see it one day:

"Now He who supplies seed to the sower and bread for food, will supply and multiply your seed for sowing and increase the harvest of your righteousness" (NASB). But until then, what do you do? Probably something similar to what I did: question and wonder when it will all be over.

Questioning God: A Normal Response

Do you have the impression that truly spiritual people never question, but are simply willing to trust God? Is that true of the heroes of our faith that we meet in the pages of the Bible? Most of those whom we regard as our heroes of the faith asked God many questions about the circumstances in which they found themselves.

Let me give you a sample of the questions they asked when God seemed silent:

How can I know? (Genesis 15:8, NIV)

Who am I? (Exodus 3:11, NIV)

What shall I tell them? (Exodus 3:13, NIV)

What if they do not believe me? (Exodus 4:1, NIV)

Why did I not perish at birth? (Job 3:11, NIV)

How long, O Lord? (Psalms 13:1, NIV)

Why, O Lord, do you stand far off? Why are you hiding? (Psalms 10:1, NIV)

Lord, don't you care? (Luke 10:40, NIV)

To question is human. When I was upset about the school situation, I questioned God. *Don't you see this problem, Lord? Why aren't you doing anything to make it change? Don't you care that Kellie is hurting? Why don't you intervene in the lives of your children?*

When we question God, we are communicating with him, we are acknowledging our relationship with him and his control over our lives. Questioning demonstrates a pursuit of knowledge and understanding. When we take our questions to God we are asking to know him better.

If you are in a waiting season, it's important that you take your questions to God. He longs for us to know him better, to seek after wisdom and understanding. I struggled through the initial months of waiting with many questions that were not answered. There was only silence. I wrote about this in my journal:

Lord, my heart is in such despair. I feel empty.... I know you are doing a deep work within me. You are wanting to heal some deep woundedness in my heart. I'm not trying to resist consciously, I'm just not sure how long all this will take and what I will be in the end. Will I get through this or will I stagger along for months in this place? Will I ever truly feel good about myself regardless of what I do? Will I ever really deeply know your goodness? Will I ever be able to accept all that you have for me without fear or doubt as to your motive?

Even though I did not get answers to these questions, I kept asking. I took comfort from the words of Oswald Chambers: "His silence is a sign that He is bringing you into a marvelous understanding of Himself. You will find that God has trusted you in the most intimate way possible—with absolute silence. If God has given you a silence, praise Him, He is bringing you into the great run of His purposes."[4]

We all try so hard to make sense of difficult circumstances by asking questions and hoping for answers. When we ask questions in general, we are sometimes seeking to satisfy our need for logical answers to illogical events. By asking these questions, we are attempting to find a way to control our future. *If I can figure out why this happened, then next time, I can avoid it.* In his book *When Heaven Is Silent*, Ronald Dunn writes: "If a logical explanation can be found, we can prevent a repetition of the tragedy. It need not happen again—especially to us."[5]

Normal questions, when directed at God from a sincere heart, can actually stimulate our faith. We may, as a result of our questions, be prompted to seek God with a fervor that was previously absent.

Heart Attitude

I think of several people I've met over the years. Some were disillusioned with God, grappling with their circumstances and questioning whether or not they really wanted to have a relationship with God. There were others who appeared to be very spiritual on the outside, going through all the right motions, but they lacked true spiritual depth.

I would much rather counsel a person in the former condition. The first person is hungering and will find a deeper relationship with God as he or she continues to wrestle with the questions. The second person is too complacent to seek more of God, satisfied, seeing no need or desire for anything more.

We need to bring all of our questions before our Father. He longs to be the one to whom we run when life makes no sense. He may not always directly answer what we're asking, but he does promise to provide himself as a refuge. "Trust in him at all times, O people; pour out your hearts to him, for God is our refuge" (Psalms 62:8, NIV). The way we weather a time of waiting will depend heavily on the questions we ask, the Person to whom we take them, and our attitude of heart.

Each of us experiences life a little differently. We may go through the same or similar experiences and react in opposite ways. Some of those differences are determined by our temperament and personality, while others may be due to the attitude of our heart.

Think of Mary and Martha, the sisters of Lazarus, who were loved by Jesus, yet were very different from each other. You may have heard sermons that contrast their two personalities, especially as related to the passage in Luke 11, when Jesus is invited to their home for dinner. But consider now the story of Lazarus' death and resurrection.

John writes that the sisters notified Jesus of their brother's illness and that Jesus stayed two days longer in the place where he was. He knew when he arrived in Judea that Lazarus was already dead, and in fact, had been in the tomb for four days. Finally, he arrived in Bethany:

> Martha therefore, when she heard that Jesus was coming, *went to meet Him; but Mary still sat in the house.* Martha therefore said to Jesus, *"Lord, if You had been here, my brother would not have died.* Even now I know that whatever You ask of God, God will give You." Jesus said to her,

"Your brother shall rise again." Martha said to Him, "I know that he will rise again in the resurrection on the last day." Jesus said to her, "I am the resurrection and the life; he who believes in Me shall live even if he dies, and everyone who lives and believes in Me shall never die. Do you believe this?" She said to Him, "Yes, Lord; I have believed that You are the Christ, the Son of God, even He who comes into the world."   JOHN 11:20-27, NASB (emphasis mine)

How would you characterize the interchange between Martha and Jesus? What is the tone of their conversation? What do you notice about the difference between Mary and Martha in this scene?

Now let's continue reading the story about Mary's encounter with Jesus:

And when she (Martha) had said this, she went away, and called Mary her sister, saying secretly, "The Teacher is here, and is calling for you." And when she (Mary) heard it, she arose quickly, and was coming to Him.... Therefore, when Mary came where Jesus was, she saw Him, and fell at His feet, saying to Him, *"Lord, if You had been here, my brother would not have died." When Jesus therefore saw her weeping,* and the Jews who came with her, also weeping, *He was deeply moved in spirit, and was troubled, and said, "Where have you laid him?"* They said to Him, "Lord, come and see."

JOHN 11:28-29, 32-34, NASB (emphasis mine)

As I read this passage over and over, I was struck that

Martha and Mary used the same words when they first saw Jesus, but the encounters with Jesus and the ensuing conversation and responses were quite different. What made the difference? I believe it had to do with their heart attitudes.

When Martha first heard Jesus was coming, she went to meet him, whereas Mary waited in the house. I consider myself a "Martha," so I surmise that, far from going to meet him out of gratitude, she went to challenge his delay in coming. The statement both sisters used, *"Lord, if You had been here, my brother would not have died,"* implies disappointment and an underlying question: "Why didn't you come sooner?" Martha responds from her head, not her heart. She goes on to say she "knows" certain truths, but I wonder—was Martha merely reciting truth? Did she really believe in her heart what she was saying with her mouth? Jesus responds to Martha where she is. He lovingly challenges her belief system by asking her what she truly believes.

Mary, on the other hand, waits to go to Jesus. When she does see him, she makes the same statement as her sister. However, she falls at the feet of Jesus and weeps. Mary responds from a humble, broken heart. Jesus responds to Mary with tears of compassion.

Martha is challenging and confrontational, while Mary is humble and responsive. Jesus, who loved both of these women, met them where they were and responded accordingly. How many times in my own life I have been a Martha, rather than a Mary. I have challenged the Lord about his delay or lack of concern, wanting him to justify his inaction. I've stated my beliefs from my head, while doubt lingered in my heart.

The difference between Mary and Martha had to do with

their heart attitude as they approached Jesus. Martha's challenging style did not put Jesus off, but neither did she allow him to meet her in the place of grief. Mary's humility not only touched Jesus, but her trust and vulnerability enabled her to receive more from his heart of love.

One book that has helped me to better understand godly waiting is Ben Patterson's *Waiting: Finding Hope When God Seems Silent*. He writes, "To wait with grace requires two cardinal virtues: humility and hope.... Only the humble can wait with grace, for only the humble know they have no demands they can lay on God and his world."[6] Mary knew what it was to wait with grace.

If you are in a waiting season, you may need an attitude check. I realized I did. I wrote in my journal:

Lord, what a purging work you are doing. I can see how I have taken pride in obeying you in deeds that are seen by others, but of more importance is a hidden obedience of the heart. I have prided myself in the "action" and fallen short in the area of attitude. I want to be a Mary and not so much a Martha.

Our attitudes will not only determine our response, but may influence where we allow our questions to take us.

Where Will Our Questions Lead?

Two summers ago, Don and I had the privilege of traveling to Singapore to conduct a series of ministry meetings. I had never traveled abroad and was a bit nervous about being in a foreign country halfway around the world. I was relieved when I found out that the church where my husband and I were speaking was made up of Chinese people who spoke English.

One afternoon we asked for directions to a store in the famous Orchard Road area of downtown Singapore. The gentleman seemed to understand our question and responded in English, telling us to go straight ahead for a couple of blocks and then turn right. We thanked him and were on our way. As we walked we realized we were going away from the central shopping area. We found our way back, but never found what we were looking for.

Later that evening, we told an American friend who is on the staff of the Chinese church about the events of the day. He chuckled a bit and said that this sort of thing was not uncommon. He explained that in the Chinese culture, it is considered shameful not to know or understand something when asked. Therefore, the people will often graciously give wrong information rather than facing the shame of not knowing or admitting they do not understand. We, no doubt, were recipients of Chinese grace!

Have you ever asked a question to have it lead somewhere you didn't intend to have it go? I find this happens a lot these days with my adolescent daughters.

I love entertaining and sharing our home with others. I'm delighted to have different friends join our family and be a part of our home life, even for a short while.

Patsy and Carol were the last of a string of visitors we'd had in our home over a six-week period. The second evening they were here, Heather was helping me in the kitchen as we were preparing dinner. Patsy and Carol were within earshot of our conversation. As Heather was peeling carrots at the sink, she said sweetly, "Mom, I love it when we have people stay at our house." I thought immediately how tender that was of her. I was smiling to myself thinking, *isn't this wonderful, here is my daughter drinking in the rich experience of having different dear friends of her parents in her home.* I was glowing inside as I thought about what precious values I was passing on to my daughter. I asked in a somewhat dreamy tone, "Heather, what is it you enjoy most about having people in our home?" She replied without hesitation, "We eat better when they're here." So much for my fanciful expectations! I glanced over at Patsy whose smile beamed a message back, "You asked her, and she told you!"

In the season of waiting which brings wondering, we may find that our questioning will lead us somewhere we never intended to go.

Downpour of Doubt

Most of us are plagued with questions that lead to doubts at some time or another. I think of Moses, who was sure God had chosen the wrong person to lead the Exodus and Gideon, who needed a double confirmation of God's call to battle. I think of Abraham and Sarah, Joseph, Hannah, Ruth, David, Jeremiah, John the Baptist, and Peter. Each of them was singled out by God, given a portion of a divine plan to follow in simplicity and trust. All demonstrated faith, but all also struggled at the core with their own humanity. It was only when they surrendered themselves to a sovereign God that the victory was won.

I find myself wanting to be like these men and women of

faith, but more often than not, I am more like the children of Israel. I long for the miraculous provisions. But when they are provided, I suffer from both short and long term memory loss. I fail to appropriate yesterday's provision as faith food for tomorrow's needs.

When the Israelites faced difficult circumstances, they began to wonder, doubt, and grumble. Just after God provided them with miraculous manna from heaven, they began to complain about their lack of water. They had eaten some of this "bread from heaven," journeyed to Rephidim, and found no water.

"Why now have you brought us up from Egypt, to kill us and our children and our livestock with thirst?... Is the Lord among us, or not?" (Exodus 17:3b,7b, NASB)

They not only questioned Moses' intent, they questioned the very presence of God, instead of drawing upon his provision, with which they were familiar.

When I face something beyond my ability to manage, I find myself questioning God's presence, motive, and character:

Lord, forgive me for challenging and questioning you in such an arrogant fashion. I guess deep down lurks the question, "Are you really good? Are you really always loving toward your children or is there a sadistic side to your nature? Even as I write those words, I see that they are not true at all of your character! But I'm not telling you anything you don't already know about how those thoughts and questions rummage around deep inside me. Cleanse me and make me able to know your truth.

Since it is not uncommon for us to wonder, question, and

doubt, the critical issue is whether or not we take all of these into the presence of God and resist the downpour of doubt which would sweep us along into the sea of unbelief. If we take them to God, he can help us to grow into a more mature faith as we quest for more of God.

Fruitfulness of Faith

How can such questions benefit our faith? Have you spent any time with an inquisitive four-year-old? They talk a mile a minute and ask a million questions. They are wondering about everything from "What are you doing now, Mommy?" to "Why can't we put the puppy in the clothes dryer after we give him a bath?" Children that age are relentless in their pursuit of more information about their world, themselves, and how life works.

So it is in our relationship with God. As we bring all of our doubts and questions before him in faith, we pursue him. We express ourselves as David did in his psalms. We pour out every question, doubt, fear, and concern to our Father in its raw form—and wait in humility.

Will all our questions be answered? What if they're not? What if the way is not made clear? What if the circumstances do not change?

We should continue to storm heaven, if we can say, with David, "I would have lost heart, unless I had believed that I would see the goodness of the Lord in the land of the living. Wait on the Lord; be of good courage, and He shall strengthen your heart; Wait, I say, on the Lord!" (Psalms 27:13-14, NKJ).

We hold fast to this hope when circumstances don't change,

direction is not clear, and questions remain unanswered. God allows us to go through wintry waiting seasons for our growth and good. They teach us to deepen our roots in faith, to hope in God, and to trust in his Word.

The fruitfulness of the waiting season is hidden from us when we are in the midst of it. Trees and plants seem to be almost dead in winter. But the long winter is part of the overall plan for harvest time. I had no idea of what God was about to do. The seeds of his plan were being sown in the garden of my heart. I had to learn to wait on him.

THREE

When Waiting Brings Wandering

Waiting does not come naturally to me. I'd much rather "do" than "wait." I find myself gravitating to tasks for which I feel I am adequate, rather than facing my own helplessness. I become easily frustrated and distracted when I'm not able to maneuver my way through to a resolution.

This is happening now, as I'm struggling to write this book. Many days I have sat at my computer without a word being typed across the screen. Every time I sit down and nothing comes to mind, I start to wander. I make a grocery list, plan my weekly menu, go to the market. I gather the laundry, sort it into piles, and enthusiastically tackle a chore I considered mundane two months ago. I clean out a drawer, walk the dog, talk on the phone, stare into space—anything but face that I'm having to wait as I write a book on waiting!

Can you relate? Do you find yourself avoiding or wandering away when you are in a situation of waiting? Do you look for a way to occupy your time so it doesn't seem so empty and unproductive? Is it difficult for you just to sit quietly before God and wait? Do you tend to stray when you face a delay?

If so, you're not alone.

Straying from God's Plan

Time after time, while Moses was leading the Israelites out of Egypt to the Promised Land, God guided and provided a way in the wilderness, only to have the Israelites wander and stray from his plan. For instance:

> Now when the people saw that Moses *delayed* to come down from the mountain, the people assembled about Aaron, and said to him, "Come, make us a god who will go before us; as for this Moses, the man who brought us up from the land of Egypt, we do not know what has become of him."   EXODUS 32:1, NASB (emphasis mine)

Notice the word *delayed*. Moses had been on the mountain forty days. The Israelites were becoming impatient, restless, doubting that he would return. They acknowledged that Moses had brought them out of Egypt (interesting note— they did not say that God had), but were disgruntled that he was not around. He'd been on the mountain for over a month without a word. He seemed to have taken God with him.

Time for a replacement, one they could see. Aaron agreed to make them a god that would be tangible, a visible representation, easily seen, and not so easily lost.

The children of Israel were caught up in the externals. When the tangible was gone and their future was uncertain, they panicked and took matters into their own hands. They began to doubt God's plan. Rather than take their doubts to him and wait anymore, they chose to abandon him and construct a god of their own preference. God told Moses:

> "They have quickly turned aside from the way which I
> commanded them. They have made for themselves a
> molten calf, and have worshipped it, and have sacrificed to
> it, and said, 'This is your god, O Israel, who brought you
> up from the land of Egypt!'" EXODUS 32:8, NASB

Aren't we tempted to do the same? I, too, become impatient when God does not answer according to my timetable. I, too, wonder where he's gone. I find myself beginning to stray; I plan ways to replace him. I want a god I can see, one who is manageable and predictable, one who can be counted on to meet my expectations. If God can't be that, I'll make one myself!

Instead of making a golden calf, I have molded my attitudes to try to circumvent the waiting season. I have fashioned these self-made idols over time and they have served me well. These become my focus and release me from having to trust a God I cannot see. Because they keep me preoccupied, I prefer to put my trust in them.

During a recent season of waiting, God began to reveal these attitudes to me. I began to understand that they were idols of my heart that needed to be purged. He showed me four idols I had run to:

- the "waiting-is-not-an-option" god

- the "do-something" god

- the "if-I-do-it-right-you-will-bless-me" god

- the "I-shouldn't-have-to-suffer" god

Refusing to Wait

As a young adult I convinced myself that God either said "yes" or "no." I did not allow that his response could be "wait." I often became polarized. It almost cost me marrying Don.

Don and I met when I was twenty-two and he was twenty-seven. I was a Christian, but I was not walking closely with the Lord. He was not yet a believer. Early in our relationship, I told him what it meant to be a Christian. Don was raised in a religious home, but had not understood his need for a personal relationship with Jesus Christ. A few days after he met me, he called his mom and said, "Mom, I met a girl I really like. There's only one problem, she's one of *them*. She's a Christian. Why does it always have to happen to me?"

After dating about six months, the Lord made it clear to me that he was calling me back to a committed relationship with him and that I needed to break off the relationship with Don. I already had had several dead-end relationships, and, although I cared for Don, I knew the relationship could go nowhere since he was not a believer.

I didn't know this at the time, but shortly after we broke up, a man named Mike, who was on the staff of Campus Crusade for Christ, ran across Don's picture in the local newspaper, cut it out, and claimed him for Christ. Don was the high-school basketball coach in town, and Mike was with a division of Campus Crusade's Athletes in Action. Mike challenged Don to meet him weekly for Bible study and Don accepted the challenge. Four months later, Don accepted Christ as his personal Lord and Savior!

Don eventually contacted me and told me of his decision. I was thrilled and reluctantly agreed to see him again, but feared he'd made a decision because of me. In the meantime, Don obtained a new teaching-coaching position and he moved forty-five miles away. He joined a church and learned more about his new faith.

Seven months after he became a Christian, he proposed to me. I was very torn. I wasn't sure I was ready to marry him, move to a new city, and quit the job into which I had been recently promoted. In addition, I wondered if he could be the "right one" since he was such a new believer. I told him I'd pray about it for a week. I prayed and fasted for several days. For me, there were only two options: "yes" or "no." I didn't even consider that God might say "wait." At the end of the week, I decided the answer must be "no" since I didn't sense a definitive "yes." I told Don my decision. Because of my rigid mindset, I not only hurt the man I loved, I almost lost him. It took two more years before God was able to bring us together.

How many other times have I delayed God's plan for my life because of my refusal to wait?

Helping God Out

You may not refuse to wait, *you* try to help God out! You make a phone call to try to manipulate a situation, drop a hint hoping someone will pick it up, pursue a course of action that may not be the best one. In any case, it's better than waiting, right?

I'm not saying that it is inappropriate to take steps when

God is leading you to do so. What I am referring to here has more to do with our resistance to waiting, which drives us to do something—anything—but wait.

Imagine how Peter must have felt when it became clear that Jesus, whom he had thought was the long-awaited Messiah, was going to be imprisoned like a criminal. Peter couldn't just wait around! No, sir, he had to *do* something, even if that something was wrong. As the soldiers of the high priest were arresting Jesus, he drew his sword and cut off the ear of a slave named Malchus.

The "do-something" god has been a driving force within me:

> *What an evil taskmaster lives inside me. My Lord cannot share my heart with such a false god as this "do-something" god! I yield over this place to you, oh Lord. Set me free from the taskmaster of control through activity. I confess it as sin and idolatry—for what has this been in my life, but that?*

Some of the ways in which I had taken matters into my own hands while waiting for Kellie's classroom situation to change were to:

- write a letter justifying my position.
- plot strategies to get my way.
- complain to others about the unfairness of it all.
- recruit them to support my cause.

You may find you have similar tactics when you face a situation you can't control. You may:

- apply short-term solutions to long-term problems.

- try to control or manipulate situations or people for selfish reasons.

- decide how God ought to deal with a person and begin the process yourself.

- see a problem and figure out how to fix it, without seeking God's counsel.

Do you carry around your own "do-something" god? Do you get busy to get your mind off the silence or the confusion? When did you last venture out to try to help God to avoid that dreaded waiting? What happened? Did it bring peace and resolve—or more frustration?

As I have found myself frantically implementing my temporary solutions just so I wouldn't have to wait for a more permanent one, I have had to decide to fire the "do-something" god and relieve him of his duties.

Performing for God

Helping God out and performing for God are evil step-sisters. Both are shortcuts to the resolution. However, performing for God has an added twist. Performing for God often comes from our distorted beliefs: we are convinced that if we perform in a prescribed manner or figure out the "right" response, God will be pleased, and will give us what we want.

Those right things often include spiritual activity: "If I would just be more committed to have a quiet time"; "If I would stop being so lazy and discipline myself to pray"; "If I could memorize more Scripture,... be more loving to my family,... help support more missionaries,... teach a class at church,... never lose my temper,... take communion regularly."

These are all fine goals. If, however, you put these expectations on yourself as a means of gaining God's acceptance and approval and make them the condition of your prayers being answered, you are caught up in performing for God.

Growing up, I felt as though I had to perform for my parents in order to be loved and accepted. I worked very hard to achieve so I would feel loved. Unfortunately, this pattern transferred into my relationship with God. I had a distorted view of God and his love for me. I have spent years trying to rid myself of this idol of performance. It has not been easy.

My parents divorced when I was five years old. My father, who is still living, told me the story of the day he packed his bag and left our home. He and my mother had been married for fifteen years but could not resolve their differences. One afternoon, I watched my dad head for the car with his suitcase in his hand. He said I stood in the driveway, crying and begging him not to leave, pleading that I might go with him. I do not remember this event, nor did I recognize the impact of that loss until God showed me how often I transfer my abandonment issues to him. I feared that God would abandon me as my father had abandoned me.

A few years ago, I wrote:

Lord, today is my spiritual birthday. Twenty-seven years ago I acknowledged my need for you. Oh, where you have brought me in that time. Thank you that your eyes have always been upon me. I know your Word says that you have never lost sight of me. Thank you for your plan in my life. Thank you for reaching down to that ten-year-old girl and drawing her to yourself.

Child, it still seems to you as though I have forgotten you at times. This is not the truth. Some of this is a result of the loss of your earthly daddy. You were confused and hurt when he left. You took responsibility for him leaving when it had nothing to do with you. You tried after that to be so good.

I still do think that way sometimes, Lord. If I'm not a good, perfect, little girl, you will leave me, too. I know this is wrong thinking, but I don't know how to manage or make sense of those times when you seem so far away. Is it I who have withdrawn from you, or have you withdrawn?

Jan, I am with you always—you have my promise on that. At times you feel less of my presence only because you have disqualified yourself from my grace.

I sometimes feel like such a failure! I do not love others as you love them. My life does not radiate your presence on a daily basis. I am helpless to produce your likeness in me.

Child, I know that, but you are condemning yourself over something that is a condition of your flesh. There is no condemnation for that which I designed. The key is the surrendering. You cannot conform your flesh, you must die to it and allow me to live through you.

Lord, I am blank. I feel deeply sad. Thank you for those who are praying for me during this time. I feel so needy and lost. So much is coming up about my father—there was nothing I could do to bring him back. I think I made a vow inside that day: "if I'm good enough, daddy will come back." Jesus, I see you there in my yard wanting to comfort that little girl who lost her daddy and doesn't know why. She's told herself if she's good and does all the right things, daddy will come back. She must not be good enough—try harder, little girl, do more, be perfect—then he will come back.

Come rest awhile, child. I know he never came for you and you have felt it was your fault. I love you so. Come rest awhile up in my arms. No need to run around frantically trying to do good—there's nothing you can do to make him come.

The "if-I-do-it-right-you-will-bless-me" god has been so deeply embedded that I still find its roots in many areas of my life. I remain grateful that God exposed this idol that had tyrannized my heart for years.

Are you stuck in a performance trap? Does it frighten you to think about what might happen if you give that up? Have you felt the frustration of its grasp in your life—always needing to do more, never good enough no matter how hard you try?

Decide now to let go of your performance-oriented habits. They won't disappear overnight, but God will indeed fill you with new life.

And if you follow my pattern, you might just have molded yet another idol from the self-righteousness you have acquired through performance. It's the one I call the "I-shouldn't-have-to-suffer" god.

Escaping Hardships

I don't know anyone who enjoys hardships. If I had, in the back of this book, included a tear-out registration slip making *you* eligible for crisis, would you send it in?

Most of us try to avoid, if not escape from, situations that cause us pain. You're probably no different. We all have a natural aversion to difficulties and hardships. The problem arises when we assume we should be exempt or when we take drastic measures to escape from situations which our Heavenly Father has allowed in order to grow us up.

The "I-shouldn't-have-to-suffer" god convinces us that we have already had our quota of hardships, or tells us we should certainly be immune since we have served God so faithfully.

Have you ever said to yourself or others, "Life is just too hard!" or "I didn't need this!"? I certainly have. And when I do, I usually try to rid myself of what I perceive to be the source of the problem or extricate myself from the situation entirely. Forget about endurance—I want *escape!* This seems especially true of ongoing or chronic problems. Some of these situations may not be gravely serious, but they are simply unending.

Just prior to leaving on vacation last summer, I had our carpet cleaned. Vacation is something we really look forward to as a family, except for one feature—where can we leave Bagel, our dog, while we are away? I hate to leave him in a kennel because he always comes home sick and flea-infested. About a month before we were to leave, missionary friends needing short-term housing agreed to stay at our home while we were away. What a relief! We left on vacation feeling all would be well.

The night we arrived home, our friends informed us that Bagel had done very well—up until a few hours before we came back. He had eaten something that didn't agree with him, and he deposited his disagreement in the middle of our freshly cleaned family room carpet, leaving a noticeable stain. Don, who is not a dog lover, was frustrated and angry. For the next two days, Bagel deposited his disagreement in several areas on the carpeted floor. I finally took him to the vet and paid $100 to be told there was nothing wrong with him.

At that point, I began to project into the future. I began calculating vet fees and carpet-cleaning expenses. I hated to think about the future stress over finding care for Bagel and dealing with my husband's frustration over owning a dog. I added up grooming costs, summer fleas, picking up "deposits," and the general care of having an animal. All of this overwhelmed me and I wanted an escape.

I thought about giving the dog away, but I knew our youngest daughter would be heartbroken because Bagel had been given to her as a Christmas gift. I thought about replacing the carpet, but knew this was impossible financially. I entertained the thought of taking Bagel back to the vet and having him put to sleep, claiming he had an incurable illness. It occurred to me that I could let Bagel run out onto a busy street, but I figured I'd end up with the vet bill and a whole lot of guilt!

Some of you who are animal lovers may be horrified by my thoughts. I was too. As my ideas became more treacherous, I realized how desperate I was feeling. When I focused on all the negatives my escapist tactics took over.

Fortunately, I did not succumb to feelings—Bagel is alive and well and lying at my feet as I write this. Some of you may be wondering, "Why in the world didn't she just get the carpet cleaned?" I did do that, but the thought of having to go through all the other eventualities over the next ten years set in motion the need for escape. *Give me a problem I can solve, but don't give me a perpetual, unpredictable condition.*

God has shown me how I have often run from hardships, rather than do the work to be willing to walk through them with him. I discovered the irony of some of my prayers in my journal:

Lord, this morning I realize how utterly childish my requests are. I want you to produce in me qualities of faith and wisdom, righteousness and holiness, but I do not wish you to take me to the places where those qualities are best developed. I shrink back when I think I must go to a place of pain, and yet, I do desire you to create in me those qualities and characteristics of Jesus. I guess that is why your Word says that Jesus learned obedience by the things he suffered. Help me not to resist your way, oh Lord, but to yield myself to you, joyfully following your call even though it appears to lead through a valley of despair. Teach me to know you more intimately. Let my flesh be surrendered to your ways and purposes. I repent of the double-minded prayers that say, "Make me a woman of faith, but don't take me to the hard places where faith is developed!"

I realized the "I-should-not-have-to-suffer" god could not coexist with the Father's will for me, which is to conform me to the image of his dear Son. I came to grips with how desperate my attempts have been to escape.

I know you have a better way, Lord—a higher plan and a deeper purpose than is readily apparent to these temporal eyes. Oh Father, how I need a heavenly perspective. Let me see with faith eyes. Develop in me strength of faith. What a paradox it is! The only way my faith will be strengthened is to be in situations where I am utterly helpless, weak, and unable to bring resolution. It is only there that I must reach highest to you, for nothing I have is sufficient to rectify the circumstance. The very thing I'm wanting to escape is the very situation that works in me the godly qualities I long for.

I now see more clearly how God has used waiting to thresh out a mindset of idolatry, which has kept me from walking more intimately with him. The threshing is sometimes painful, but its purpose is clear. God wants us to know him and to bear fruit. He will lovingly prune, thresh, or root up anything that threatens his harvesting the garden of our hearts.

God causes us to wait for our good, to manifest his glory in and through us. As I have re-read my journals, I am in awe of how God has answered the deepest cries of my heart, even in the midst of my wondering and wandering. Maybe you have identified with my wanderings. Have you strayed from God's presence? His plans? Do you recognize any idols you have formed to alleviate this waiting process? Are you willing to forsake those idols and learn what it means to be stayed upon God? If you are, he is willing to meet you.

Staying Upon God

There is a wonderful verse in Isaiah that may serve to anchor our souls as we drift in the sea of wandering:

> Who is among you that feareth the Lord, that obeyeth the voice of his servant, that walketh in darkness, and hath no light? Let him trust in the name of the Lord, and *stay upon his God.*   ISAIAH 50:10, KJV

This word *stay* in the Hebrew means to "lean, rely, or support oneself upon." It suggests a total reliance on God. Notice that the verse indicates there will be times of darkness, even for the one who fears the Lord and obeys him. We all face these times when our vision is limited and we lack clarity with regard to God's intended direction. But in those times, we must learn not to fashion for ourselves our own idols, as did Israel, but to anchor ourselves in God.

I've been told a ship in the midst of a storm at sea cannot chart its course. It must look for a landmark, a lighthouse, on which to focus. The ship's captain must head for the light as much as is possible, even though the course may not be straight. He needs an immovable focal point.

The third verse of John Wyeth's hymn, "Come Thou Fount of Every Blessing" always brings tears to my eyes:

> Oh, to grace, how great a debtor,
> Daily I'm constrained to be.
> Let Thy goodness, like a fetter,

Bind my wandering heart to Thee.
Prone to wander, Lord, I feel it,
Prone to leave the God I love;
Here's my heart, O take and seal it,
Seal it for Thy courts above.

I am keenly aware of my tendencies to wander—to stray from God's presence and his plan, and to give allegiance to the false gods of my own making.

What do we need when we have a bent toward wandering? We need to be anchored, held to something solid or Someone who is immovable.

The writer of the letter to the Hebrews uses the phrase, "an anchor of the soul" (Hebrews 6:19, NASB). When we fix our eyes on him and place our hope in him, it means we stop depending so much on the externals, refuse to rely on our self-made idols, and trust his plan.

One day, I was reflecting on how Jesus calmed the storm on the lake (Luke 8:22-25):

Lord, I see how in a storm I use different skills and personality traits, how I have prided myself on being able to muster the courage to meet the storm head-on. But how very weak and powerless I am to face aimless waiting!

I see how it is futile to apply the same tactics and techniques I use in times of storm-tossed crisis as I do in times of waiting. They effect no change and only exasperate and exhaust me. I know you are trying to teach me how to rest and wait in quietness and confidence. Help me not to fight you, Lord, but to learn to be tranquil in this place. Teach me, oh Lord, to have faith in this place of the unknown.

Charles Spurgeon wrote of "standing still and seeing the salvation of the Lord":

> What, if for a while thou art called to stand still, yet this is but to renew thy strength for some greater advance in due time.[1]

The waiting season affords us such opportunities. Richard Hendrix said,

> Second only to suffering, waiting may be the greatest teacher and trainer in godliness, maturity, and genuine spirituality most of us ever encounter.[2]

Has God delayed his answer in your life? Instead of wandering aimlessly, will you set your ship in his direction today? You may feel as though you are drifting amidst a sea of waiting. Determine to focus and be stayed upon your God. He will bring you to your desired haven!

FOUR

When Waiting Brings Whining

～×～

Several years ago I was traveling by plane to Toronto, Canada for a television appearance. We had to go through Chicago's O'Hare International Airport. A blizzard had just hit the area. As we boarded the plane, we were assured that we would get to Toronto that evening. We sat on the runway for four hours with nothing to drink or eat because they contended we would be leaving at any time.

Finally, around midnight, they brought us back into the terminal because Toronto had a curfew and would not allow us to fly in after midnight. I was tired and just wanted to get my luggage and find someplace to stay. We were told the airlines would not be covering hotel accommodations because the delay was due to weather. There were over one hundred very disgruntled passengers expressing their discontent. "Why did we sit on the runway for four hours? What do you mean you're not responsible? Now it's after midnight, and we have to try to find somewhere to stay. We've had no food or drink and you're not offering compensation!"

The final straw came about 2 A.M. when we were told we could not get our luggage because there was no one to unload it from the plane, which meant we had to wait for another three hours until the next shift came on. A riot nearly ensued, and I was among the rioters. Sarcastic comments were flying, people were flinging out barbs and insults and questioning airline personnel about their integrity. By 5 A.M. I was exhausted—and convicted about my actions and remarks. I hoped no one would ask me where I was going. After my earlier performance, I could just imagine myself smiling sweetly and saying, "Oh, I was going to Toronto to appear as a guest on a Christian television program. You see, I'm a Christian author and speaker."

When circumstances are difficult or uncomfortable for me, I am often tempted to gripe and complain. I am so uncomfortable when I have to wait... even when God is the one who has kept me waiting. I forget so quickly that he knows what he's doing—in fact, I feel *most* frustrated when I have to wait God. I react the most strongly to this God who is so uncontrollable and unpredictable.

Like a toddler who is angry because her mother won't let her have a cookie, I have thrown tantrums when God didn't change a circumstance or explain it to my satisfaction.

The Desert of Discontent

The Israelites did the same when God did not do what they wanted him to do. Despite all that God had done for them by miraculously delivering them from slavery and death in Egypt, the children of Israel were quick to murmur and complain at the first sign of difficulty. Several times, the Israelites complained about their lack of provision, but each time God met their need in a loving, miraculous way. When they complained about having no water, God sweetened the bitter water at Marah and then gave them water from the rock at Horeb (Exodus 15:25 and Exodus 17:6). When they lamented about finding no food in the desert, he sent them manna in the morning and quail in the evening (Exodus 16:4, 12-13). When they questioned his presence, he appeared in a pillar of fire by night and a cloud by day to guide and comfort them (Exodus 13:21-22).

God was extremely patient with their griping and complaining when they first came out of Egypt. It's as if God were dealing with them as young children, in the early stages of learning to walk with him. But later, as recorded in Numbers 11, he dealt with them more severely, because it was time for them to grow up.

It's Time to Grow Up

Strange, isn't it—we can so clearly see the immaturity of the Israelites' response to God and remain blind to our own? How many times I have responded to God like the whining Israelites! I recorded my struggle in my journal:

Lord, the words "it isn't fair" just keep echoing in my heart. It isn't fair that when you're good you still have to suffer and endure hardship. I think of Joseph, Job, Jesus—all who did the right and pleasing things and yet, they still had to suffer. Where is the justice in that? Doesn't your Word teach that as we are obedient to your ways and statutes you will bring us prosperity and blessing?

Child, child. Blessing does not always come in the form you suppose. I see things so much deeper than your vision allows you to see. I bring far greater blessing than the temporal external things you see with your eyes.

I'm tired, Lord. It feels like you've tricked me. I've served you and obeyed and you've brought me to a hard place. I don't like to hurt or go through these places.

I am trying to free you, child. You must come to the place of knowing my goodness and my kind intent toward you. Jan, there is no cruelty in my heart toward my children. This is so different than what you have known. Those seeds of cruelty have taken a deep root in you and have produced a distorted view of my character. I am good and loving and kind. There is no maliciousness in my nature—only goodness and gentleness toward my little ones.

But Lord, where is the fairness and justice? How can you allow such things to take place in the lives of your children? How can you see the pain they suffer without intervening sooner?

Just as your heart ached for your precious Kellie this morning, so my heart aches for my own.

But Lord, you have the power to change things. I don't, and if I could have made her well this morning I would have.

It is in my heart to bring to you good things. I cannot explain my ways to you for you are limited in your ability to see. This is where faith comes in.

Oh Lord, increase my faith.

I had been accustomed to God's responsiveness and I wanted him to continue to deal with me as he had in the past. He had always seemed so near and available. I would pray about something and the answer would be there. Now, I was entering into a maturing phase in my relationship with him. He was still very present in my life, but it seemed as though he'd withdrawn himself. I wrote more:

"I will never desert you nor will I forsake you." This is your promise, Lord, and you are faithful to your Word no matter what I may feel inside. You will never abandon me. You are here and promise never to leave me. It seems that some of these truths that I have known so long are only now sinking into the depths of my spirit. Let me cling to your truth, Lord. Let me learn to walk and live in the knowledge of your constant presence—I need you.

You need not go anywhere to find me, child, for I am here. There is nowhere that I am not present, for I will never, never, leave you. Oh, how I have longed for you to know this truth. Reach out your hand and find me there. I am constantly abiding with you, even though at times you feel as though I am nowhere to be found. My Word is true—nothing can separate you from my love— not even your feelings.

In this desert place, God was trying to teach me about his provision. My whining was starting to give way to acceptance—of manna and quail and sweet, sweet water.

Seeing God's Provision

Instead of looking at the desert as a place of God's provision, the children of Israel had looked at it as a place of deprivation. They could not see past their discontent to rejoice in the provision God was faithfully giving them day by day.

I didn't know I needed to learn this until I was in the midst of my desert place:

"The Lord will be a stronghold in times of trouble" (Psalms 6:10). Lord, I feel so foolish, because from all appearances this should not be a "time of trouble" in my life, and yet there is an inner storm. Please guide me now. If there are steps you want me to take, show me. If I am just to be in this place, then allow me to grow and learn what you are trying to teach me. I must know your peace even before the circumstances change. I want to know your love deep in my heart. I am helpless to muster it up inside. It is not a brainwashing that I need, but a renewing of my mind. You need not demonstrate any more of your love for me, for I have all the evidence in the world. I just can't seem to incorporate that truth in my innermost being....

Jan, you've learned to base things on the outward appearance.

Lord, you have so many times demonstrated your love to me in ways others would long for. Yet, this is not reaching my heart. Somehow it seems empty now. Why is it?

Child, you can't live on yesterday's manna. I am trying to teach you of my daily provision for you—not the past or future provision, but only what I have for you today. I want you to walk with me today, to know my mercies for you are new every morning.

I guess I'm afraid, Lord, that the manna will not be there tomorrow, and then what will I do? Please help me, Lord, to accept your daily provision with gratitude. I'm not even sure, Lord, how to gather the manna for each day.

Jan, each person was only required to gather as much as he and his household needed. You have often come to me gathering for others and not gathering for your own nourishment. That is why you are depleted and weak. You cannot gather manna for others outside your household for I have made provision for them as well.

After I received this insight from God, I did some reading about God's provision of manna in the wilderness. Manna sustained the Israelites for forty years. It needed to be gathered daily and could not be stored (except on the sabbath). As I inventoried my life, I realized that often I tried to store up yesterday's manna—trying to live off what he had done instead of meeting each day. I realized that God was trying to teach me how to gather his provision for myself daily. I also needed to learn what my "manna" looked like, before I could gather it and use it for my nourishment.

In addition, I saw how many times I had gathered spiritual food for others. I would go to the Word, anticipating upcoming speaking engagements. I would be reading with someone else's need in mind. As a result, I felt undernourished and even a bit burned out in ministry.

G. Campbell Morgan wrote, "That is the peril of the age in which we live. We may be so busy running on His errands and attempting to do His work as never to sit still and look into His face."[1]

He is our source for everything, every day.

Not Quite What We Expected

There are times in a desert of discontent when our continual complaining results in God giving us exactly what we've asked for, but we find out it is not what we really wanted.

The children of Israel realized something similar. They complained to Moses about God's lack of provision for them. Even though God had faithfully rained manna from heaven, they were dissatisfied. They complained by saying, "If only we had meat to eat! We were better off in Egypt!" (Numbers 11:18, NIV).

The Lord told Moses to tell the people that he would give them meat to eat, but that they would not eat it for "just one day, or two days, or five, ten or twenty days, but for a whole month—until it comes out of your nostrils and you loathe it—because you have rejected the Lord, who is among you, and have wailed before him, saying, 'Why did we ever leave Egypt?'" As a result, God drove quail inland from the sea and the people began to eat, but "while the meat was still between their teeth and before it could be consumed, the anger of the Lord burned against the people, and he struck them with a severe plague. Therefore the place was named Kibroth-hattaavah (graves of craving), because there they buried the people who had craved other food" (Numbers 11: 33-34, NIV).

I haven't managed to do any better than the Israelites did. When I realized that I was weary of a ministry of speaking and traveling, I started complaining to God. I was tired of the phone calls, the travel preparations, the airport hassles, the people who clamored for my attention, and the lonely hotel rooms. God answered my prayer one weekend while speaking at a conference. I was sitting by the Chesapeake Bay enjoying the cool breeze in my hair and watching the pleasure boats on the glistening water. The Lord seemed to say:

Child, I want you to have a time of rest—a place of cool refreshment where we can meet. You're like a ship that I am calling to harbor. But you fear that you are past your time—that you will never set sail again. Do not fear, my child, for this is a time of replenishment for you. A time of refreshing. Open every portal, every door, that I might bring you peace and refreshment. I have only called you away for a time. When you set sail again you will be empowered by the renewing and transforming work I have done in you while you were on the shore.

God had answered my prayer. I really didn't know how long this would last, but I eagerly looked forward to a time of restful refreshment. What I encountered, however, was a "wrestful renovation" that lasted far longer than I wanted!

In the middle of my respite, I was hit with depression. Although I had complained about being tired when I was traveling, I now missed the adulation, the activity, the "strokes" I had received through performing that role. I realized how much I lived for the spotlight. I had had difficulty developing a mature, consistent walk with God, but I had been able to ignore it because I had been so busy.

God used this time of waiting to thresh and winnow impurities that had mixed with the good grain in my life. He taught me to move from my fleshly responses to waiting, to "active waiting." I needed to learn what it truly means to wait on God. I had a lot to learn about being content in his provision.

You may have caught a glimpse of yourself. If you're a complainer who is wandering through the desert of discontent and at a dead-end, it is not too late. God wants to teach you to cultivate contentment—even in the desert.

Cultivating Contentment

Spurgeon wrote:

Covetousness, discontent, and murmuring are as natural to man as thorns are to the soil. We need not sow thistles and brambles; they come up naturally enough, because they are indigenous to earth; and so, we need not teach men to complain; they complain fast enough without any education. But the precious things of earth must be cultivated. If we would have wheat, we must plough and sow; if we want flowers, there must be the garden, and all the gardener's care. Now, contentment is one of the flowers of heaven, and if we would have it, it must be cultivated; it will not grow in us by nature; it is the new nature alone that can produce it, and even then we must be specially careful and watchful that we maintain and cultivate the grace which God has sown in us."[2]

How do we foster contentment? How do we make it grow? Is contentment a natural trait or can it be cultivated? How does one become more contented? One thing is clear: Cultivating is not a one-time act, but a continual, repetitive process. In order to be content, we must choose to cultivate it in our lives over a period of time.

Paul writes, "I have learned to be content whatever the circumstances" (Philippians 4:11, NIV). The word Paul uses here in the Greek for "learn" means "to learn by use and practice, to acquire the habit of, be accustomed to."[3] In other words, Paul did not come to be content one day forever and always. It was something he acquired over time by active practice.

We all need to uproot the weeds of complaining and put genuine effort into *learning* to cultivate contentment. Consider these steps:

1. In order to cultivate contentment, we must have a willing heart. We must remove any stones of bitterness, discontent, or fear that might prove to be an obstruction preventing contentment from taking root in our hearts. We must be willing to turn up the soil and remove any contaminants which would poison the blossoming of contentment.

2. We must take time to plant the seeds of contentment in our heart's garden. We must pause and take notice of things in life for which we are thankful. We must learn to savor those precious moments when we are at peace with God, in spite of the circumstances around us. We plant the seeds of thanksgiving which will bring in a crop of contentment.

3. We must water our seeds of contentment with the Living Water of God's presence in our lives. As we come to the "fountain of living water" we will be continually cleansed and refreshed. His watering will keep the seeds of contentment from drying up and becoming brittle. We must come often to the water source to drink in his life-giving presence.

4. We must remove the weeds. I learned recently that there are different kinds of weeds. There are annuals or perennials. "Annuals respond to regular hoeing. Perennials must be removed carefully, roots and all, or they will be that much more resistant next year."[4] There are sometimes stubborn patterns in which we have persisted for years that will take some time to change. We need to continue to root those up from the garden of our hearts with God's help, so as not to choke out the seeds of contentment.

5. Feeding the seeds of contentment with the Word of God will cause your garden to flourish. A regular feeding is necessary for the seeds of contentment to grow up to maturity. The Word will multiply the fruitfulness of the seeds sown and will produce a harvest beyond your expectations.

Have you grown discouraged and tired of waiting? Do you feel parched and dry inside? Have you spent too many lonely days in the desert of discontent? Do you long to know the peace and contentment Jesus offers? If so, claim the promise God gave to Jacob—and to me: "I will go down to Egypt with you, and *I will surely bring you back again*" (Genesis 46:4, NIV).

Let those words wash over you and refresh your spirit. Your Father has not forgotten you.

FIVE

When Waiting Brings Wallowing

From the time Don and I met, he'd always had aspirations of being a basketball coach on the college level. He had turned down a recruiting position at a four-year college the year before we married, but I knew one day he would have the position he hoped for, because he was a good coach who believed in teaching good fundamentals of basketball (and life) to his athletes.

A year after we married, he applied for a job at a local junior college. He did very well in the interview and was complimented by the athletic director, who told him his reputation of excellence had preceded him. The director had had several phone calls from other coaches who attested to Don's knowledge of the game and character. But Don did not get the job. This was the first in a series of job interviews that did not come out as I expected. I had prayed as each one came up, hoping each would be *the* one.

Several years ago, Don was offered a part-time head coaching position at a junior college with the understanding that the position would be made full-time the following year. Although it meant a grueling schedule, Don took the job and was very successful. In the spring, several other job opportunities opened. We began praying for God's direction. He was interviewed at a private college, and was asked if he would take the job if it were offered. We discussed it together and felt as though he should wait for the full-time position to open where he was. There were other tenuous circumstances that were not in the best interest of our family, and so Don declined.

Shortly after this interview, he was interviewed for another junior-college position that was part-time. We struggled to know which way God was leading. Don was really wanting a full-time position which meant he could primarily coach and not have to teach at the high school and then travel to another location to coach a team. He was offered this job, and was very torn. At first, he said yes, but the more he prayed the more he wondered if he had made the right decision. It was in a better location as compared to where he was, but we kept thinking his current position would be full-time, as he had repeatedly been assured that a full-time position was in the making for the following year.

I prayed diligently for days, asking the Lord to give Don wisdom. We both agreed there were positives on both sides. After more prayer, Don informed the college that he would not take the position, because he really wanted to simplify his life by working in one place. The next day I got a call at home from his present employer.

"Has Don already turned down the other job?"

"Yes, he just told them yesterday. Why?"

"Oh dear." My heart sank as I heard the following words. "I just found out the position here will not be full-time next year. In fact, we're not sure that it will ever be full-time due to all the budget cuts."

I burst into tears. Don came home a few minutes later and I told him the news. He could hardly believe it. We were both in shock. He immediately phoned to see if the second position had already been filled. He was told it had. The interview committee had an unprecedented Sunday meeting and called another coach who accepted the job. Don hung up the phone in bewilderment.

I felt devastated and tricked. *How could you have let this happen, God? We asked you to show us and now look what has happened. We prayed and sought you with all of our hearts and you did not warn us. Is this the way you treat your children, when they have faithfully sought you for wisdom?*

I took it much harder than Don. All the past years of disappointment over his job situations boiled to the surface. Many times I had stuffed down the disappointments in my heart and kept a record of them. Because I had not brought them all before the Lord, they remained buried and had sprouted into a bramble of bitterness.

I felt betrayed and angry; in fact, I was wallowing in my bitterness for months:

Lord, I just want to learn whatever it is I'm supposed to learn so I can move on. It seems as though you are leaving us hanging. There seems to be no clear direction for us. It's so scary trying to discern your will. Will I interpret things incorrectly? There are so many questions weighing on my heart. Please do not leave us alone to try to figure it all out. You say in your Word that if we ask for wisdom you will give it. When your children ask for bread you will not give them a stone. But dear Father, we have sought you and still every-

thing seems foggy. Help me to know you and your peace in the midst of the fog.

Child, child, child, I know you are anxious and desiring to know the way. I am not holding back from you as you suppose. I desire to delight your heart. Yet, there are things that must be purged away for you to receive the fruit of the land.

Lord, how long? It feels like I will never be good enough, just like at home when I was a girl—my parents held things out in front of me, never intending to fulfill the promises. The promises were made only to secure my obedience and performance. Is that the kind of Daddy you are, Lord? I know in my heart you are not, but it feels so much the same. That's where the root of bitterness and anger resides in me—"never good enough," "work harder." Dear Jesus, free me from this bondage and lie. Forgive me for feeding the root of bitterness in my heart. It was true in my family, but it is not true of you. Show me your character—teach me of your goodness and faithfulness.

In his classic book, *A Shepherd Looks at Psalm 23*, Phillip Keller offers a picture of what wallowing looks like. He describes a sheep that is "cast" as one "that has turned over on its back and cannot get up again by itself. A cast sheep is a pathetic sight. Lying on its back, its feet in the air, it flays away frantically struggling to stand up, without success." Apparently, sheep become cast when they "lie down comfortably in some little hollow or depression in the ground."[1] If the shepherd does not find them in time and assist them to their feet, they will die.

Our wallowing has the same result. The more we lie in our particular wallowing place, the more difficult it becomes to get back on our feet.

Where Do You Wallow?

Waiting seems to bring wallowing, especially when we feel out of control. Most of us have several favorite wallowing places: self-pity, complacency, anger and bitterness, doubt and unbelief, just to name a few. Which do you gravitate toward?

Have you ever wallowed in an attitude of self-pity? Bitterness? Anger? Hopelessness? Doubt? You probably did not intend to get stuck there; it just happened. My friend Sy Rogers says, "Whatever we feed grows stronger, but whatever we starve, grows weaker and eventually dies." Have you fed an attitude that has now become a rut or a way of life for you? If so, you may be wallowing.

Maybe you're not the angry or bitter type, but like Vicky, your wallowing is subtler:

I received a call from Vicky several years ago when I was conducting a support group for women with abusive backgrounds. Vicky called to express interest in joining our group and I interviewed her on the phone to assess her readiness. As we talked she told me about her past and all the people who had hurt her. She blamed her unhappiness on people in her past. I told her that the goal of our group was to help women work through their hurts. I shared with her from my own life, telling her that this process took time, but it was possible to get beyond the pain and anger. Vicky expressed interest but shared that she'd gone to a number of groups and that the last group had asked her to leave after attending one time. She said, "I suppose you'll reject me, too."

Vicky was content to stay a victim and continue to blame others for her problems. A classic wallower, she had no intention of working through her issues to bring herself to a resolution. She only wanted a new audience.

Complacency. A.W. Tozer wrote, "Complacency is a deadly foe of all spiritual growth."[2] Complacency is a "self-satisfaction accompanied by unawareness of actual dangers or deficiencies."[3] When we wallow in complacency, we're satisfied to stay put and feel offended if anyone challenges us.

Sometimes we confuse waiting with wallowing in complacency. We don't want to make any effort to change and are committed to being comfortable. Vicky wallowed in complacency.

If you see that you sometimes become stuck or complacent, consider these wise words from Eugene Peterson: "Waiting does not mean doing nothing. It is not fatalistic resignation. It means going about our assigned tasks, confident that God will provide the meaning and the conclusions."[4]

Self-pity. Vicky also wallowed in self-pity. She went to group therapy in order to rehearse her condition over and over, hoping to draw attention and sympathy. People who wallow in self-pity believe their plight is worse than anyone else's, and they usually reject any proposed remedies. They only see the negatives.

The children of Israel had a few complacent, self-pitying "wallowers." They had limited perspective and had a flair for self-inflicted martyrdom. In Numbers 13 and 14 the Bible describes the period of Israel's history when the twelve spies were sent out to scout out the land of Canaan. Although God had promised this land to Israel, ten of the twelve spies came back with a negative report. The ten spies painted a bleak picture, saying Canaan was a land that "devours its inhabitants" and they compared themselves to "grasshoppers" in the sight of those who occupied Canaan. Even though Caleb and Joshua urged the people to reconsider because of God's promise and their favorable discovery about land that flowed with "milk and honey," the naysayers prevailed. They complained to Moses and Aaron saying, "Would that we had died in the land of Egypt!" (Numbers 14:2, NASB).

Doubt and unbelief. Israel not only made excuses about why they couldn't enter the promised land, but suggested among themselves they appoint a new leader who would take them back to Egypt! They were not only shrinking back from taking the step of faith, but were also thinking about regressing to the old way of life! Their wallowing was rooted in doubt, doubt of God's promise.

My wallowing often has a lot to do with my belief system. I "roll around" in many distortions which lead to doubt about God's goodness and his promises. Part of God's purpose in the waiting was to expose many of those distortions of his light and truth.

When God is silent I am tempted by false notions about him that begin to take root in my heart without my knowledge. My journal reveals what God was kindly teaching me through his silence:

Am I holding onto bitterness toward you, Lord? Help me to work it out. I hear a little girl's voice inside me saying, I obeyed. I did what you told me to do, and you haven't kept your part. I've done the hard things and remained faithful to what you said, but you have not fulfilled your promises.... Lord, the adult in me knows the time must not be right, and that I can trust you. But I confess the child inside feels betrayed, let down.

Have you ever felt like you were being "set up" or tricked by God? I had been a Christian for nearly twenty-five years, but God was needing to bring to my attention many distorted beliefs about him and about myself. For a long time I had been unaware that these beliefs existed and were affecting my ability to walk in greater intimacy with God. God began to reveal where some of these distortions came from.

One Christmas, when I was nine years old, my sister and I begged my parents to allow us to open a present on Christmas Eve. At first, my stepdad said no, but my sister and I were relentless. Finally, he agreed with one stipulation. He got to pick out the present we were to open. We agreed happily and could hardly wait until dinner was over that evening.

I'll never forget how very excited I was to open a present. My stepdad handed me my package and I opened it furiously, ripping off the paper on a shoe box. I lifted the lid—to my utter dismay, there in the box was a pair of my old worn-out slippers. I was devastated. My stepdad laughed hilariously. I was deeply disappointed and humiliated. How could I have hoped for something good? Later we were given other gifts to open, but the sting of the cruel trick had already burrowed its way into the depths of my heart.

The Lord brought this memory to mind, along with others, to show me when and how some of my distorted beliefs had come into being. I was not aware that these beliefs had embedded themselves in my heart, but the Spirit of God knew, for "he searches our hearts" (Romans 8:27, NIV). Once I recognized them, God could begin to replace them with truth.

This process can be painful, too painful to endure in a short time, and our Shepherd knows we need time to grow in his grace. Therefore, he initiates a season of waiting for us, a time of working on the issues as he directs.

Depending on God's Promises

Depending on God's promises almost always means we must take our eyes off the externals and exercise faith. It means we rely on, trust in, and adhere to his promise in the absence of what we can see, touch, or feel.

This has been difficult for me at times, because I have so depended upon my own abilities to evaluate situations by what I see. I have frequently struggled with depending on God:

"What we call the process, God calls the end. What is my dream of God's purpose? His purpose is that I depend on Him and on His power NOW. If I can stay, in the middle of the

turmoil, calm and unperplexed, that is the end of the purpose of God…. It is the process, not the end, which is glorifying to God.[25] *Oh Lord, how many times I've taught this concept and yet have not applied it in my own life! It is not the product, but the process you delight in. Please don't let me miss you in this process. I am so anxious to have this season of waiting over so that I can get to the "goods." Forgive me for not living in the now—trusting your provision NOW—experiencing your love NOW—living in contentment NOW—abiding in your peace NOW. I confess to you that this is one of the most uncomfortable places for me. I want to move on into the promises without living in the faith and assurance of the promises today…. I guess what you are trying to teach me is how to seek you each day, each moment, with every situation and circumstance. I get so scared in that place, Lord, for fear I might miss you or not do the right thing.*

Jan, it is not up to you to figure this out. You are still depending too much on yourself instead of learning to rest and abide in me. Even in your caution you rely on yourself rather than me. I am calling you to total abandonment.

Lord, I'm not sure what that means or even how to do it.

It is not a "doing," child, but a "being." It is a relinquishing of self, and the pressure you put on yourself to "do it right."

What if I am wrong, Lord?

What if you are? Am I so small that I cannot turn anything to my ways? You have underestimated my power and overestimated your own. No one can thwart my purposes.... Jan, I *am* able to keep you.

Our ability to depend on God is directly correlated to how we view Him. Dr. David Seamands, noted author and speaker, wrote:

The most determinative factor is our "feltness" of who God is and what He is like. It is surprising the number of genuine Christians who are caught in an inner conflict between what they think about God and what they feel about God.... Years of experience have taught me that regardless of how much correct doctrine Christians may know, until they have a picture and a felt sense that God is truly good and gracious, there can be no lasting spiritual victory in their lives.[6]

As I have reiterated, I have found it difficult to overcome the less-than-ideal father images which have colored my picture of my heavenly Father.

One morning, the Spirit of God seemed to speak to me and say, "Jan, you've come to know and trust Jesus in your life, and you've incorporated the Holy Spirit, but I am going to take you on a journey of knowing the Father." I wish I could tell you I was excited at that moment. In reality, I was scared to death. It was true that I had spent most of my prayer life focusing and addressing my prayers to Jesus and desiring more of the indwelling presence of the Holy Spirit.

But I had systematically shied away from praying to the Father because I didn't want to invest any effort in developing a more intimate relationship with my Abba Father.

Now I partially understand why God needed to take me through a season of waiting. It helped me to acknowledge my distortions about God as Father and grieve through the losses of my childhood. Then, as I emptied my heart and mind of those distorted images and idols, Father God began revealing more of his true Father's heart to me, as I was willing to open my heart to him.

I believe I will be in this process until I see him face to face. You may be at a crossroads yourself. You want to depend on God, but the doubts overwhelm you. You find yourself wallowing in your unbelief, afraid to step out and rely on God. He will not force you to trust him, he will only invite you.

You may wish to echo one of my prayers. I recorded it after two years of waiting. His winnowing wind had begun to blow in my life.

Lord, you are doing a deep work within me and have a greater plan than I can see. I miss the sureness of your guiding light in my life and the sweetness of your presence. You are weaning me from all the externals that I had come to trust. I know you have called me to this place and that this is your appointed time. But everything inside me feels so at odds—so contradictory. I trust you are going to produce a good work in me. I wish there were another way all this could be accomplished, but I do trust you to choose the kindest, yet sharpest tool to do the necessary surgery in my soul. Oh Father, please do the work necessary, no matter how much I kick and scream, rant and rave. I do desire to have all that you want for me. I wish I could be weathering this pruning process with more grace....

If that is your prayer, he hears you. He wants to make you holy. Take heart. It is essential that the grain of your life and mine be threshed of all the stalk and chaff. Remember his Word promises not to keep you there a moment longer than necessary. He is faithful to complete the work he has begun.

Listen. Do you feel the rising breeze? The winds of the Spirit are gently blowing. There's a refreshment awaiting. Come to the threshing floor, the winnowing work is about to begin.

PART TWO

God's Winnowing Wind

SIX

When Waiting Brings Wrestling

"**D**on, I can't believe she would not budge!" I fumed as I reviewed my meeting with Kellie's principal. "She said she was not able to accommodate my request due to classroom size. Honey, you're a teacher. Could she not add one more student if she wanted to?"

Don agreed that it seemed as though something could be worked out. He promised to call the next day and talk with the principal. In the meantime, I was churning inside. I desperately needed to protect my little girl, but my efforts were futile. Kellie's situation was triggering in me emotions which had long been buried. It was reminding me of every time I didn't feel protected as a child. I wondered why God was not working this out:

Oh Lord, I so want to give Kellie what she needs—what I never got. I know what it's like to live through a situation where you have no control. You learn how to get by, how to adjust... and hope dies inside. Everyone is telling me, "Give it time, give it time." Don't they understand that time is what makes the hopelessness set in? "She'll adjust," they say. I know she will, because I did, but is that what we want her to do?

Jan, you can give Kellie all the love and support you never received, even though the situation does not change.

But Lord, will she feel all the things that I felt? Will she feel I just gave up and did not protect her and see to it that she was not hurt?

Jan, you cannot be everything to her. You are to be my heart, arms, mind for her, but you cannot be her God. You continue to love her, to pray for her, to point her to me. Jan, she will not feel all those things that you felt if you will support her and love her. What she will learn is that you are human and that moms are not the ones who can do all and be all. You both must seek strength and understanding from Someone beyond yourselves.

I was wrestling with emotions that were bigger than the circumstance warranted. I've discovered this is often the case. When our emotions are more intense than the situation demands, they are triggered by issues rooted in our past. God's desire was that I not miss this deeper work of healing internal wounds because of my quick-fix mentality. I needed to be thrust into a time of wrestling with these issues; I needed to wrestle through a waiting season.

What does it mean to wrestle through the waiting season? It means that we actively take part in what God is trying to work in and through our lives. We come to him in all of our humanness, with humility, bent on actively pursuing his intentions. In doing this, we may find ourselves wrestling first with our circumstances and then with our emotions, wrestling for control or comfort. Eventually we may realize we're wrestling to know God.

What is Wrestling?

What picture comes to your mind when you hear the word *wrestling*? Do you imagine two opponents on a wrestling mat, each in a contorted position? Or do you see someone wrestling an alligator? Do you envision a person who is having an obvious internal struggle?

Wrestling, by definition, means to "engage in deep thought, consideration, or debate; to strive earnestly as if in a violent or determined struggle."[1] In my case, the situation with Kellie became the initial focal point of my wrestling. I struggled with how this could have happened and attempted to find a way out. Most of us probably do this. When life issues us a circumstance that is contrary to our expectations, we immediately fight it.

Wrestling With Our Circumstances

I think about the many times I've been speeding along the freeway and then—oh no!—a traffic jam. It always happens when I'm supposed to be somewhere on time. I wrestle with the frustration of being stuck. As I'm crawling along the freeway and then come to an exit ramp, I wrestle with a secondary dilemma—whether I should stay on the freeway or exit to surface streets and contend with their numerous stop lights.

You may be in a circumstance right now that you're wrestling with. You may have lost your job, had a miscarriage, struggled for years with a chronic illness, or lost a loved one.

It is perfectly normal to wrestle in these situations.

I think of our friend, John, who lost his wife suddenly on Valentine's Day. His wife Tina had contracted a heart infection that had not been detected. They had risen early that morning and spent time in devotions together. John got the call later that morning that Tina had collapsed at work and had died. They'd been married a little over five years. John wrestled in the early months following Tina's death. *How could this have happened? We've been faithful to the Lord! How could a loving God allow this?*

Most of us think of Jacob when we think of a scriptural character who "wrestled." But don't forget another person who wrestled: Hannah. The Bible tells us that Elkanah had two wives, Peninnah and Hannah. Peninnah had borne children for Elkanah, but Hannah was barren because "the Lord had closed her womb." Each year, Elkanah would observe the yearly sacrifices and travel to Shiloh. He would take along Peninnah and their children and Hannah. He gave leftover sacrificial portions to Peninnah and the sons and daughters, but to Hannah, he gave a double portion because he loved her. However, this did not compensate Hannah for her barrenness, because Peninnah would "provoke [Hannah] bitterly to irritate her, because the Lord had closed her womb" (1 Samuel 1:6-7, NASB). Hannah was so distressed she wept and would not eat.

Finally, one time, she went to the temple to pray. She made a vow to the Lord that if he would hear her prayer and give her a son, she would dedicate him for life to the Lord's service. Eli, the priest, was observing Hannah as she prayed. When he saw her lips move but heard no words, he rebuked her for being drunk. She explained that, far from being drunk, she was a woman "oppressed in spirit" (1 Samuel 1:15, NASB). This caused Eli to bless her with a favorable benediction, asking the Lord to grant her petition. She went away with hope and worshiped the Lord the following day. Soon after their arrival home, Hannah conceived; nine months later, she gave birth to a healthy son, whom she named Samuel. After the child was weaned, Hannah made the trip to the temple and there presented Samuel to Eli and the Lord, making good her vow.

Hannah's life offers us a real-life picture of waiting with weeping and wrestling. What can we learn from her?

We're told Hannah wept and poured out her soul in grief before the Lord. *What have I done to deserve this? Why is God not changing my plight?* She must have wrestled over God's silence, year after year, as her rival Peninnah continued to bear children and taunt her. "O Lord of hosts, if Thou wilt indeed look on the affliction of Thy maidservant and remember me, and not forget Thy maidservant, but wilt give Thy maidservant a son, then I will give him to the Lord all the days of his life" (1 Samuel 1:11, NASB).

Are you wrestling with circumstances beyond your control? Why does God not answer, if he is in control? The situation you are in has continued far longer than you ever anticipated. You have searched your heart to see if there is unconfessed sin. You have pounded on heaven's door, but no answer has come. What possible good is coming from this season of waiting? What is there left to do?

I can't answer all those questions for you, but I can tell you this: one of the greatest gifts God has given us is freedom to express ourselves to him without fear of reprisal. As we wrestle with our circumstances, it is also all right to wrestle with our emotions, out loud, before him.

Wrestling With Our Emotions

How many times did Hannah pray over her condition?

Was it the sixtieth or the six-hundredth prayer that God finally answered?

Is there a formula for prayers that ensure God's quick answer?

We often ask ourselves such questions in an attempt to resolve what can only be trusted to God. Our emotions run high as we wrestle with our difficulties. We know that God is aware of all we think and feel even before we utter a word, but in his tender mercy, he invites us to bring it all into his presence. He wants us to "draw near with confidence to the throne of grace, that we may receive mercy and may find grace to help in time of need" (Hebrews 4:16, NASB). He invites us to come without pretense.

He is careful to hear us and teach us. As I have learned over the years how to wait and listen, he has been faithful to teach me and comfort me in all that I have wrestled with before him. Are all my prayers answered according to my desires and timetable? Usually not, but I continue to wrestle, asking God to give me a heart like Hannah's.

We read Hannah's words in 1 Samuel 1:15: "I have poured out my soul before the Lord" (NASB). Wrestling means we *pour out our souls* to the One who longs to be gracious and have compassion on us. It does not guarantee an immediate end to the waiting. It does promise to bring a deeper work inside us.

As you read this next entry from my journal, think about whatever circumstance you are in that is the focus of your wrestling. Allow God to use these words to minister to your heart as he wills:

> You know, child, this is just not about Kellie. I am trying to teach you of my love for you as well. Even though I do not always change things in your life, it is not because I don't love you. It is because I see a higher good—I see beyond what you see. You have long battled this road. I want to teach you the peace your heart has longed for **before the resolution comes.** I want you to know me in the midst of what appears to be hopeless. I want you to provide Kellie with what I wish to provide you. Sometimes you fight me on this because you do not wish to accept what I will not change.

> *But, Lord, a good daddy would see how very hurtful this is to his child and he would do something to make it better.*

> You are right, my child, but all your life you've thought that the solution was to change or rectify the circumstance. What I am trying to teach you is that good daddies don't always change things and take away the pain. They provide love and comfort in that place. If they always changed it, my children would never know how to cope or comfort others.

Lord, there's a part of me that's mad—I don't want the peace to endure it, I want it to change.

Jan, this is the very reason I have placed you in these situations—you are resisting my way.

But Lord, if I rest in that place, doesn't it mean that I have given up?

There is a difference, my child, between giving up and surrendering. **Giving up is often from exasperation and a sense of no hope. Surrender is a peaceful letting go that is surrounded by strength and confidence.** You have often confused these two, even as my servant Peter did. This is why I have had you on this road. I know it is hard for you—for I am the one who formed you in your mother's womb. I am the one who has made you to possess the perseverance and tenacity in your nature. **I am also the one who is calling you to rest and surrender.** It is not a lesser road—as I have told you, it is one where no flesh can glory. You have prided yourself on qualities I am now asking you to lay down—not because they are unusable, but because the journey I am taking you on requires a different set of qualities. **I am going to teach you perfect peace and rest in the midst of calamity.**

Wrestling is often the first stage of surrender.

So what circumstances are you wrestling with? Are your emotions in turmoil? Do your prayers seem to fall on deaf ears? You approach an anniversary or a reminder date that leaves you despairing and hopeless. As painful as it is, I encourage you to pour out your soul to God. Wrestle with your emotions before his throne. Pour out your soul as Hannah did. Ask the Lord to lead you through your struggle to surrender, because, when you think about it, what you are really wrestling for is *control.*

Wrestling for Control

Most of us want control, but would not know what to do with it if we got it! I think of the many times I've been on an airplane in turbulent air conditions. I've wanted to be in control so that queasy feeling in my stomach would disappear. The truth is, if the pilot were to summon me to the cockpit and hand over the controls, I'd be in far worse shape.

Why do we so persistently wrestle with God for control of the circumstances in our life? I don't think most of us would really want control if he gave it to us. We do want to dictate outcomes and timetables, and prevent hardships—all without carrying the full weight of our decisions. Like some young adults who still live at home, I want all the rights of an adult in my Father's house, but none of the responsibility. I want the right to determine my course, but I want God to take charge of making sure it all works out just right!

What leads us to believe we can take control effectively? Our evaluation system is so faulty. Only God's is perfect. He "sees a higher good," and can "see beyond what I see." "For as the heavens are higher than the earth, so are my ways higher than your ways, and my thoughts than your thoughts" (Isaiah 55:9, NASB).

We evaluate our circumstances with limited vision. We determine a situation to be good or bad, right or wrong, fair or unfair, a blessing or a curse, as we sift it through our limited understanding. Richard Foster summed us up well when he wrote, "Frequently we hold on so tightly to the good that we do know that we cannot receive the greater good that we do not know. God has to help us let go of our tiny vision in order to release the greater good he has in store for us."[2]

At times I have wondered if God really is in control. It is difficult to believe he is sovereign when I look around and see the evil and pain all around me. It is even harder for me to believe when that pain touches my life or someone I love. In such situations I wrestle with God for control. I clamor for a pain-free existence.

Wrestling for Comfort

In Psalm 73 we read that Asaph struggled with these issues as well. He said "For I was envious of the arrogant, as I saw the prosperity of the wicked. For there are no pains in their death; and their body is fat. They are not in trouble as other men; nor are they plagued like mankind" (Psalms 73:3-5, NASB).

He was troubled as he looked around and found there to be no justice. He continued by saying, "Surely in vain I have kept my heart pure, and washed my hands in innocence; For I have been stricken all day long, and chastened every morning" (Psalms 73: 13-14, NASB).

I have felt that way. Like Asaph, I have pondered these things and they have only created more questions and, at times, disillusionment. I've looked around and compared myself to others, feeling as though God had singled me out. I've even asked God how he could let so-and-so get away with such-and-such as long as he has. I accuse: "Are you really in control, God? Do you really see what is going on here?"

But for Asaph there was a turning point. He said, "When I pondered to understand this, it was troublesome in my sight until I came into the sanctuary of God" (Psalms 73:16-17a, NASB).

As long as we are looking outward trying to reconcile what we perceive in the flesh, we will always come up wanting. We will interpret our hardships and trials as God's displeasure or an attack from the evil one. But when we can with faith-eyes focus our attention on God and rest in his sovereignty, we will come to a place of peace. At the end of his psalm Asaph writes, "But as for me, the nearness of God is my good; I have made the Lord God my refuge, that I may tell of all thy works" (Psalms 73:28, NASB).

What is it that Asaph could "tell"? If God did not change his circumstances, what was there worth talking about? It is God's nearness and comfort *in the midst* of these hardships that brings peace, not the resolution of the situation. That is why Asaph could say that he had made God his refuge. That is why he had something to tell.

When I give up wrestling for control and comfort and in faith exchange my finite vision for God's eternal perspective, I experience a peace and comfort beyond any temporary satisfaction I might find in a life filled with ease. It's true. The one who knows the greatest peace and comfort of the harbor is the one who has been shipwrecked by the raging waves.

God never promises us smooth sailing or a pain-free existence. In fact, Jesus promised just the opposite! He said, "These things I have spoken to you, that in me you may have peace. In the world you have tribulation, but take courage; I have overcome the world" (John 16:33, NASB).

Whether you're wrestling for comfort or for control, or you find yourself wrestling with your emotions in a painful circumstance, God wants to be your refuge. He wants to lead you to "nestle, not wrestle," as Corrie ten Boom used to say. But the process takes time.

At some point, we reach the most crucial time of our wrestling. It is where we wrestle to know God.

Wrestling to Know God

As I waited for God to answer my prayer for Kellie, I realized how much I still wrestled with the question: Is God *really* good?

My answer would determine my response to life's external events. If I believe the answer is, "No, God is not good," I will continue to try in my old self-determined way to resolve external events. If, however, I believe the answer is, "Yes, he is good," I can trust in God's sovereignty with all the externals and learn to surrender.

God knew those doubts still lingered in my heart and he wanted to expose them to the light of his truth. I had often been caught up in the externals of life and had missed the internal workings of God's Spirit. My struggle over my inability to control Kellie's circumstances brought me to the place where I could see my questions about God's goodness. Up to that time they had existed outside my conscious awareness.

As a result, I began searching the Scriptures for verses that spoke of God's goodness and his sovereign nature. I read and reread Psalm 78, which is a record of the history of the nation of Israel and God's compassion for them. I memorized verses from Psalms 106, 107, and 136, all of which declare God's goodness and lovingkindness. Eugene Peterson writes that we should not hesitate to put any Scripture passage under the searchlight of our disbelief. He contends that "the reason many of us do not ardently believe in the gospel is that we have never given it a rigorous testing, thrown hard questions at it, faced it with our most prickly doubts."[3]

I wrestled for months with the incongruity in my heart.

Father, how I need to know your Daddy's heart of love. I see it clearly in Don's eyes when he looks at our girls. Let me know you in such a way—to know your intent is always good and not evil. That your heart aches when I ache, that you grieve over what makes me sad—that you delight over what brings me delight. I confess that I don't know your heart. I still have fears. Forgive me and correct this image.

I know, child, that you struggle to know my true character and nature.

How am I to know it, Lord? How will it ever be a part of my heart? I confess that I fear what you have in store for me. But your Word says there is "no fear in love." I want you to implant your love into my heart. You have already proven yourself to me over and over again, and yet I always ask for more. Oh, how I wish I had had a positive experience with "fathers" so that it might not be so hard to make that truth a reality in my life. I'm so sorry I see you differently than you really are. I know it must sadden you, as it does me when my children misunderstand my intentions. Oh Jesus, I need to know the Father as you do!

Where will wrestling take us? God knew that this season of waiting would produce a wrestling which would ultimately lead me to an intensified pursuit of him. He knew I would wrestle to know him more intimately than ever before. "Sometimes the very place God brings us to is the place where we know the greatest hunger. What we do with our hunger as we wait is crucial."[4] I wonder if God does not allow these times in our spiritual lives to impassion our pursuit of him.

As I look back over the years, I see how much my focus has changed. My quest to change my circumstances has gradually shifted to my pursuit of knowing God more intimately. The irony of this is that God has been more elusive to me than ever before in my life. There have been long periods of silence, times of loneliness, a seemingly joyless existence, a desperate seeking to know him and his will for my life.

In all of this, I know God is at work to answer the deepest cries of my heart, even when I get sidetracked. He hears and remembers our petitions, and often, through the waiting season transforms and purifies our longings to reflect more of an eternal quality.

It's worth it. It wasn't until I began writing this book that I realized the truth about wrestling: it is an essential part of waiting. Ben Patterson writes: "To wait on God and to pray is to wrestle with bewilderment and perplexity. But it is God himself who brings on the bewilderment and perplexity. He does it that he might cause us to so encounter him and wrestle with him that we come to know him as we never have before. It is his way of making us come to know more deeply his goodness and mercy."[5]

Wrestling brings us to a deepening of faith, a realization of our helplessness, and an awesome reverence for our God who knows our frailty and folly. Our capacity to love God and be loved by him is being expanded, deepened, broadened. Were it not for the waiting and wrestling, we would be like a seed planted in the soil that is content to remain there, never reaching upward for sunshine or downward for nutrients deep in the soil. We might be comfortable, but we would never fulfill our intended purpose or divine potential. As we wrestle in waiting we break away from complacency and enter into companionship.

Grace-filled waiting is really not just waiting at all. It is about knowing God and becoming intimately acquainted with him as a Person and discovering the expansiveness of his redemption. It is about grappling with unknown circumstances while grasping for the One we know, but do not fully understand.

Waiting and wrestling through what seems to be a hopeless or unknown situation and struggling to hang onto a thread of faith when there is little else to cling to is part of the journey of walking with God. When we really know him, we need not be caught up in the "whys" of his purpose and "whats" of his plan.

We are like wheat which has to be threshed and winnowed. In Bible times, after the initial threshing, the good grain was piled in a corner on the threshing floor to await the evening breezes. Although the stalk had been removed, there were still traces of chaff and straw that had mingled with the good kernels. The evening breezes allowed the harvester to take a winnowing fork, tossing a portion of the grain in the air. As he did, the lighter chaff would be blown away, while the heavier seed would drop to the floor to be gathered. This process would be repeated several times to guarantee that all the impurities were removed and only good seed would remain. The good seed was gathered and stored and used to provide food for the sustenance of life.

Do you desire to be used in service for his kingdom? All believers who are seeking God will be threshed, winnowed, and poured out. The harvest season in us is followed by a threshing and winnowing process because, as "wheat," we aren't yet "edible." Even though God has removed some of our more obvious sins, there still remains chaff in our lives that must be purged and separated from us if we are to be life-producing agents in the service of our God. The evening breeze used to separate the chaff from the wheat is symbolic of the work of the Holy Spirit in our lives. He continues to blow his refining wind through our lives to remove all the debris. This is sometimes time-consuming, but God knows exactly what is needed to accomplish this purifying work in our lives. Isaiah 28:24-29 (NASB) says it beautifully:

Does the farmer plow continually to plant seed? Does he continually turn and harrow the ground? Does he not level its surface, and sow dill and scatter cummin, and plant wheat in rows, barley in its place, and rye within its area? For his God instructs and teaches him properly. For dill is not threshed with a threshing sledge, nor is the cartwheel driven over cummin; but dill is beaten out with a rod, and cummin with a club. Grain for bread is crushed, indeed, he does not continue to thresh it forever. Because the wheel of his cart and his horses eventually damage it, he does not thresh it longer. This also comes from the Lord of hosts, who has made His counsel wonderful and His wisdom great.

This is comforting to me; God will not keep me in the waiting season one moment longer than necessary.

I can now see that my inability to control Kellie's situation was merely the external event God used to bring me to the place of wrestling through internal issues that were far more significant. God's divine threshing tool—waiting—separated the stalk from the good grain of my life and winnowed the chaff that had mingled with his good seed in my life.

Is God threshing you as you wait and wrestle? You can help the process if you remember to share with him your doubts and fears about his sovereignty, and confess your need for control and comfort in whatever area you find you are hanging on. Don't be afraid to wrestle with your circumstances and emotions in his presence.

And wrestle to know him more intimately. Pursue him, even if it means you must wait. Cling to him, even when the silence is deafening. God wants to draw you closer. Jesus understands. He went to Gethsemane's garden to pray. He knows the agony of wrestling, the anguish of weeping, and the joy that comes from willingness. He will meet us there.

SEVEN

When Waiting Brings Weeping

I had little understanding of what it meant to garden until recently. I've learned from my twelve-year-old daughter that this arduous task takes more than just digging a hole and dropping in a few seeds. It requires soil preparation, choosing a proper location, watering, weeding... and waiting, with no guarantee of a result.

Kellie is a horticulture enthusiast. Last November she secured a plot of land for a yearly fee at our local university's arboretum. The day after she chose the plot she asked if we could get to work clearing the land so she could begin planting. She could hardly wait to get started. I've been amazed at how much I have learned as I've watched my child pour her heart into this fifteen-square-foot piece of land.

Kellie and I worked over three hours in her garden yesterday. The ground had compacted due to our dry, warm weather. We could not even plant the few flowers and vegetables we had bought that morning, because the soil was too hard and dry. Kellie and I had to spend the first two hours watering and turning over the soil in preparation for planting. I reflected on how many times my heart had been in such a condition. God was not able to sow in my life, because I was hardened and not receptive to his seed of truth.

Weeping Softens Our Hearts

Do you see the parallel with our heavenly Gardener? To soften and break up the ground of our hearts in order to make it more receptive to his seeds, God can use our own tears. Sometimes he has had to rain adversity on me to bring me to the point of weeping, but that weeping has softened the soil of my heart, breaking me open to receive the seed he desires to sow.

"That's a nice image," you may say. "But what's the point, beyond getting the seed into the unyielding soil of my heart?" Growth, of course, and a promised harvest. When we sow in tears, we are breaking up the hardened ground of our hearts and inviting God to sow seed which will reap an eternal harvest. The eventual *reaping* is the point of today's *weeping*.

Until recently I've always had difficulty understanding Psalm 126:

Those who sow in tears will reap with songs of joy. He who goes out weeping, carrying seed to sow, will return with songs of joy, carrying sheaves with him.

PSALMS 126:5-6, NIV

What works the transformation? What does "seed" correspond with in my life? What "sheaves" can I expect to bring home?

Eugene Peterson offers some insight into these questions. He writes:

The hard work of sowing seed in what looks like perfectly empty earth, has, as every farmer knows, a time of harvest. All suffering, all pain, all emptiness, all disappointment is seed: sow it in God, he will, finally, bring a crop of joy from it. It is clear in Psalm 126 that the one who wrote it and those who sang it were no strangers to the dark side of things. They carried the painful memory of exile in their bones and the scars of oppression on their backs. They knew the deserts of the heart and the nights of weeping. They knew what it meant to sow in tears.[1]

So does my friend Carol. One of her adult sons died two years ago in a tragic accident. She is still grieving his death. She told me about another mother who was losing her daughter to cancer, and said, "I don't have any words for her as we talk on the phone. Sometimes I just listen and weep with her." Both of them are sowing in tears. One day, they will reap in joy. And to Carol's credit, even before her own time of weeping is past, she is willing to help another fellow-sufferer "sow in tears."

Oh, How We Resist!

How long has it been since you wept? Perhaps you are resisting your need to cry. Many of us run from the cleansing, releasing act of weeping.

I allow myself to cry more than I used to. Many of you are the opposite—your tears are held back behind a dam of self-control. My tears have often come as I've waited for God in a situation that seemed hopeless. Other times I have been brought to tears through loss or grief. But even a "weeper" knows what it feels like to resist crying for fear of breaking down too much and becoming vulnerable.

I find it remarkable that even though Jesus himself mourned with tears, many within the Christian community set their jaw in opposition to this practice of "godly mourning and weeping." In our culture, we seem to have lost the significant practice of mourning and weeping. This lack has taken a toll on us physically, emotionally, and spiritually.

> Today, there no longer is a socially established period of mourning. We have moved into a phase of almost denying its existence. Often, it is expected by friends and relatives that the bereaved "be strong" and not show any signs of grieving. Our more popular way of thinking of bereavement is that grief is a sign of weakness. To the contrary, showing emotions and grieving at the time of a loss is a healthy and appropriate way to get through the transition towards the building of a new life.[2]

We read of several times in the life of Jesus when he was "moved with compassion," and two other specific times he was moved to tears. One is in John 11, when Jesus was brought to the tomb of Lazarus:

> When Jesus saw her [Mary] weeping, and the Jews who had come along with her also weeping, he was deeply moved in spirit and troubled. "Where have you laid him?" he asked. "Come and see, Lord" they replied. Jesus wept.
>
> JOHN 11:33-35, NIV

The Greek word used here means that Jesus shed tears, weeping silently.[3] We must assume here that Jesus was not weeping over Lazarus' death, for he was about to raise him from the dead. But rather, Jesus was responding in compassion to the agony experienced by those who had lost someone they loved. He did not rebuke them, but entered into weeping with them.

We also read in Scripture about Jesus' triumphal entry into Jerusalem:

> As he approached Jerusalem and saw the city, he wept over it.... LUKE 19:41, NIV

The Greek word here means "to sob or wail aloud."[4] This type of weeping was a public expression of intense grief or mourning. Here Jesus modeled for us the poignant weeping that comes from the very pit of our stomach. Truly, Jesus was a God-man of sorrows and acquainted with grief (see Isaiah 53:3, NASB).

Many of us must pass through the place of mourning and weeping as we journey toward obedience to God. Jesus himself "learned obedience" (see Hebrews 5:8) with anguish. Scripture tells us that Jesus passed over a brook called Kidron on the way to the Garden of Gethsemane. As Jesus was praying in the garden, he was in "anguish and his sweat was like drops of blood" (Luke 22:44, NIV). In the Hebrew, *Kidron* is derived from a word which means "to be ashy, dark-colored, or by implication suggests a place of 'mourning.'"[5]

Waiting and weeping go hand-in-hand. We might weep over our losses, our limitations, or our failings. We sometimes weep for joy even though our waiting time is not over.

Weeping Over Losses

For our tenth anniversary, Don surprised me with a beautiful half-carat diamond solitaire pendant. He'd been planning for months to present me with a gift that would represent our loving relationship. He drove into Los Angeles, carefully chose the diamond, and kept all of it a secret until our special day. I was overwhelmed by his tender expression of love to me.

Every day when I put the pendant around my neck I was blessed as I thought about how God had redeemed our relationship over the years. Both of us had come from a hurtful past and had spent the first few years of our marriage struggling through the baggage we'd brought into our relationship. Finally, after ten years we were beyond those early challenges and were enjoying each other and celebrating our love and life together.

Late one evening while on a speaking engagement in Canada, I came in to my hotel room after a full-day seminar. I was weary and wanted to collapse before my early flight out in the morning. As I prepared for bed, I took off my pendant, and slipped it into my jewelry pouch, making a conscious decision not to leave it on the nightstand for fear I would leave it. I left the zipper of my jewelry pouch open, intending to pack everything in the morning. When my wake-up call came in the morning it was still dark outside. I got ready, packed my things, and went off to the airport.

Back home a few days later, I went to put on my pendant and discovered it was missing. At first, I thought it had slipped out and was probably in the bottom of my suitcase.

When I couldn't find it, panic set in. I retraced my steps. Could I have left it on the nightstand? No, I distinctly remembered putting in my pouch. *Oh no!* I thought. *I wonder if in my haste in packing, it fell out. I do remember that zipper being open.* I phoned the hotel immediately and told the manager about the situation. He agreed to get back to me.

In the meantime a torrent of emotion hit me. *"Not my diamond. Not this, Lord. Oh Lord, it is too precious. It can never be replaced. Lord, let them find it. Don't ask me to give that up. Please, Lord, I beg of you, not this."*

I called my best friend, Ginny. I was so upset she thought someone had died. It was something so precious to me—so symbolic. It was hard to put into words to try to explain to another human being. Ginny understood because she knew my background. My anguish reflected the wounds from my past. My loss brought back all the emotion I had felt as a result of my childhood losses.

Don comforted me the best he could. I walked around my house for three days, grief-stricken. I would be making dinner, folding the laundry, or going from one room to another, when all of a sudden the weeping would start. I imagined the hotel maid must have found it; she was wearing my husband's love around her neck!

I pleaded with God to intervene. But by the third day, I knew it was hopeless. My diamond was gone—forever. As I cried, the Lord spoke to my heart. He simply said, "There is nothing that you've lost that I will not redeem to you." Even God's words seemed empty to me as I touched my bare throat.

I had called our insurance company about the loss. At first, it appeared that there would be no compensation, but there was a turn of events. The insurance company listed the loss as a theft, obtained replacement estimates from several jewelers, and issued us a check authorizing replacement.

Because we went to a wholesale dealer to replace a pendant that had been appraised at retail cost, my new pendant was twenty points larger than my old stone. As Don clasped my new pendant around my neck, I couldn't help but think about the Lord's words to me. The pain of the loss was still there, but it was as if God was comforting me by replacing my loss with something exceedingly abundantly above what I could ask or think.

Warren Wiersbe writes:

[God] not only knows your tears, but He records them and retains them! Why? So that one day He may transform them into *gems* of joy and glory. No tears are ever wasted when you follow Him [emphasis mine].[6]

As I reflect upon the tears I've shed, I can't help but wonder if when I get to heaven I will see bottles and bottles of diamonds, transformed by my King, who is ever faithful to redeem to us all that has been lost.

All of us are acquainted with loss. Loss is a part of the human condition. We lose a friend, a pet, a job, our health, or—hardest of all—a spouse or a child. "We experience loss whenever we lose or are deprived of something or someone we value and have become attached to. The loss may feel like a tap on the shoulder or a two by four across our forehead.

The severity of the impact depends on the significance of the loss."[7] When we are faced with deep loss, we are catapulted into a crucible of grief, drenched in tears. God has equipped us with the ability to weep to help us process our losses.

Weeping is sometimes talked about in terms of "breaking down." When we weep, we are vulnerable, and vulnerability is scary. Over the years, I have met so many men and women who have avoided their tears for various reasons: "It shows I'm weak," "It hurts too much," "I'm afraid I'll never be able to stop," "I feel stupid," "It does no good." The years of locked-up emotions have taken their toll on them, often through physical pain, emotional detachment, or spiritual indifference. Sometimes a circumstance arises which breaks through our resistance.

When Rod Carew, baseball Hall of Famer, lost his eighteen-year-old daughter to leukemia, he said, "I've become more emotional. I never showed emotion before, no matter what I was going through, but since my daughter has gone through this I've cried more and opened up more to people I know care about me. Before, I would have just shut everyone out." Carew further revealed that he had always been distant from the media and that he "shunned publicity" due to the fact he had been abused as a child and "hated bringing back bad memories." Due to his daughter's illness, "Carew began to warm to the public and he let others warm to him."[8]

Many times, griefs help us to be receptive to the heart of God and the needs of others. Through the loss of my pendant, I was able to grieve at a deeper level the losses of my childhood, more fully embrace the love of God, and increase my understanding of God's ability to redeem all things. Grieving through my own losses has helped me more effectively minister to others who have experienced loss. My weeping helped this to happen.

Remember Hannah? She poured out her heart to God and "wept bitterly." She was grieving over her barrenness. But out of that circumstance, God brought redemption for Israel through a child named Samuel. We cannot always be assured that weeping over our losses will result in exactly what we desire, but we can be confident that he "is able to do exceeding abundantly beyond all that we ask or think, according to the power that works within us" (Ephesians 3:20, NASB).

As you've been reading, the Holy Spirit may be bringing to your mind some of your losses, maybe something from your past or maybe something current. As you bring those losses to him, know that his heart is tender toward you. His Word promises that he makes "all things new" (Revelation 21:5, NASB). Don't be afraid to shed tears and vocalize to God your loss.

In addition to weeping over our losses, we may also find ourselves weeping over our limitations.

Weeping Over Limitations

What are your own limitations? Are there things you used to be able to do that you can't do anymore, like stay awake after 10 P.M. at night?

Because of a back injury, Don has waited through chronic pain. The injury occurred in high school, over thirty years ago. He has undergone two back surgeries and has received injections, physical therapy, medication, prayer, and the laying on of hands. But despite all efforts, he can no longer lift, run, or sit for prolonged periods.

Several years ago when our children were younger, friends who had a swimming pool frequently invited us over to swim. Our host was a very active man who loved to play with the kids. He would get right in the water with his two children and our two daughters and would become a human spring-board. He would position the kids on his knees and thrust them forward into the air with all of his strength. The kids loved his "jet job."

Don would enjoy watching his girls having so much fun, but it was bittersweet for him. He wished *he* could be the one in the pool providing fun for his girls. He couldn't even carry them into the house and gently place them on their beds when they fell asleep in the back seat on the way home from such an outing.

Waiting often forces us to face some of our own limita-tions. We can't make things happen even when we try our hardest. The longer we wait, the more aware we become of our powerlessness.

As I discovered, I was powerless to effect even a simple classroom change for Kellie. I wept for frustration at my inability to resolve her painful circumstances. Nothing worked. My mother's instincts were thwarted. Often, it is such ordinary experiences of our helplessness which drive us to a more earnest pursuit of God.

I think God allows us to experience our own limitations so that we might turn to him and acknowledge his qualifications. Those of us who have the motto "when the going gets tough, the tough get going" find it especially painful facing our limitations. There I was, a mother with a concerned heart, a professional counselor married to a professional teacher, and all my qualifications were ineffectual.

I think of the apostle Peter. He felt he was highly qualified as Jesus' disciple, immovable in his devotion. He declared his loyalty by saying, "Even if all fall away, I will not" (Mark 14:29, NIV), and, "Lord, I am ready to go with you to prison and to death" (Luke 22:33, NIV). Unfortunately, Peter placed too much emphasis on his own capabilities. He did not fully abandon himself to God until after he had denied even being acquainted with his beloved Lord.

How often have I convinced myself that "I can handle this one on my own," only to face the humiliation of failure. God takes no delight in embarrassing me, but he wants to show me my need for him and demonstrate his all-sufficiency. I should have learned this lesson by now! A friend of mine used to say, "God will take you around the mountain once, and I hope you will learn the lesson the first time. But just in case you don't, be assured he'll take you around as many times as necessary to bring you to the place of total abandonment in him."

Peter learned his lesson well. His tears were "good seed," sown in a field broken up by his awareness of both his limitations and his failure.

Weeping Over Our Failings

What must it have been like for Peter when he heard the cock crow?

According to Luke, "While he was still speaking, a cock crowed. And the Lord turned and looked at Peter. And Peter remembered the word of the Lord, how He had told him, 'Before a cock crows today, you will deny Me three times.' And he [Peter] went out and wept bitterly" (Luke 22:60-62, NASB).

I can only imagine what he must have felt inside. Beyond forgiveness. A failure. Worse than an enemy to his Beloved. He had failed, and failed miserably. Rugged Peter, who had boasted of his courageous devotion, had denied his Lord when challenged by a simple maid.

Earlier, Jesus had told Peter, "Simon, Simon, behold, Satan has demanded permission to sift you like wheat; but I have prayed for you, that your faith may not fail; and you, when once you have turned again, strengthen your brothers" (Luke 22.31-32, NASB). I find this passage encouraging. Jesus knew how miserably Peter would fail. This failure did not *disqualify* Peter from service, but in fact, Jesus prayed that it would be used to *qualify and equip* him. Jesus wanted to transform Peter into a rock of strength for other believers. Carsten Thiede comments:

Not only has he failed his Rabbi and Lord whose prophecy has now been fulfilled; he has also given the lie to his bold statement of some hours before, that he would never disown him. The man who wanted to prove himself rock is shattered to pieces. He had to be broken by his own powerlessness before satanic temptation in order that he could be made whole.... his betrayal demonstrated utter human frailty, against which the forgiveness of Christ would shine even brighter. If Peter could not only remain, but properly *become* the rock of the Christian community after such depths of faithlessness—how much greater was and is the hope for ordinary men and women, believers as well as not-yet-believers, that God will patiently forgive them their sins![9]

Don't put Peter in a class by himself, some kind of special category of person. Jesus "lives to make intercession" for all of us, and "he is able to save forever those who draw near to God through him" (Hebrews 7:25, NASB). Take a minute to consider your experiences of life. In what areas do you feel as though you've failed? What has contributed to your assessment? Have you ever wept bitterly over any of these failings? Have you talked to the Lord about your failings in these areas, or have you just tried to ignore them?

Acknowledging Our Failures

Most of us would rather not face our failings. We'd like to ignore them or sweep them under the rug. But we have all had to come face to face with our failings at one time or another. God wants us to embrace our shortcomings and sins and respond to them in repentance. It is what we do with them that counts.

Not long ago, I found out my oldest daughter had lied to me about something. I disciplined her by restricting her phone privileges and denying her permission to attend some extracurricular activities. She cried excessively over the situation, but it was apparent that she was far more upset over the consequences than she was over having lied. Being a typical parent, I went into a lengthy discussion (Heather calls them lectures) about the difference between remorse and repentance. I told her remorse is feeling badly when we get caught dong something wrong and have to pay some consequence for our actions. Repentance is a genuine sorrow over the wrong with a desire and motivation to change.

Heather appeared to be listening, but I suspected that most of my words were going in one ear and out the other. About two weeks later, I overheard her talking to one of her friends on the phone, who evidently had been wronged by another friend. "You know, Emily, just because she's apologized doesn't mean she's really sorry. There's a difference between feeling badly about something when you get caught and truly feeling sorry from your heart for what you did. It's the difference between remorse and repentance...." I caught a glance from my daughter as I walked by and I smiled. Later on that evening, she said, "See, Mom, I really was listening!"

Of course, I can't remember even my own good advice sometimes. As I face my failures and sins, my waiting seasons have been anything but "graceful" on my part, but ever so "full of grace" on God's part.

A few years ago, my journal was full of entries concerning my failings. It seemed as though all I was doing was weeping over sin and confessing. I wrote:

Lord, the more I wrestle, the more I come to understand how absolutely powerless I am to make myself different. I imagine Peter faced these same realizations through his failures. It is a dying to self and pride. Help me lay down my efforts, with hopeful expectation. It feels as though I'm failing you, but I'm beginning to see that this is exactly where you've wanted me to travel. You are taking me to the end of myself that you might really have all of me and demonstrate your power.

I read parts of Job last night and this morning. Lord, you have shown me how my heart has been filled with rebellious pride. I have not acknowledged your awesome holiness or your sovereignty. Instead, I have challenged your nature and demanded things of you. Please forgive me and wash me, even as Job said, "I retract and repent." How patient you have always been with me, Father. I feel so ashamed that I did not weather this season well.

Child, don't you know that I know all that is in your heart? You have only disappointed yourself. You are learning that apart from me you can do or be nothing. It is my Spirit that works in you all good things. As you surrender to me, I am raising you up to be all that I created you to be.

Grief and sorrow become a divine rendezvous with the Prince of Peace, the Father of mercies, and the Spirit who "intercedes for us with groanings too deep for words" (Romans 8:26, NASB). Paradoxically, our most treasured times become not the mountaintop experiences, but the valleys of despair.

Nevertheless, I still find myself presenting my case to the Lord, contending I am a much better mountain climber than valley trekker! I'd rather weep for joy any day!

But I do know that we cannot truly weep for joy until we have wept for sorrow.

Weeping for Joy

A scene that is indelibly imprinted in my mind is the labor and delivery of my first child, Heather. Like most American first-time parents, Don and I attended classes to help prepare ourselves for the delivery. We decided to learn natural childbirth techniques.

After fourteen hours of labor at home, we went to the hospital. After about three more hours, I was hooked up to a machine which would monitor my contractions. Don held my hand gently and read portions of Scripture to me, trying to prepare me for the next contraction. I remember thinking to myself, *This is too painful, I want to get out of here. Time out—I want to call this off!* Don was reassuring me, "You're doing great, sweetheart. That's it, just keep counting. Just a few more seconds. There, it's almost over now. Good. You made it. It's over now. Lord Jesus, help Jan make it through this pain." No choice. I had to wait it out, weathering the pain.

I was finally wheeled off to the delivery room where I was instructed to push with what little strength I had left, surrounded by cheerleaders whose repertoire included only one cheer, "Push harder, now. You can do it!" Before long, I saw the doctor hold up the most precious sight I'd ever seen. "It's a girl" he said. Instantly, both Don and I burst into tears of joy. Our child was born. She was beautiful. The waiting was over. The effort was finished. The pain was gone.

Don later asked me if the tears of joy were due to the pain finally being over or because she was born. I told him there was a little of both, but the abundance of the joy did not come from that moment alone. Seeing Heather was the culmination of many months of waiting with anticipation. At her birth, the joy sprang out, but it originated in the time of waiting and all that it included, both the discomforts and the eagerness.

> Blessed are those whose strength is in you [Lord], who have set their hearts on pilgrimage. As they pass through the Valley of Baca [tears], they make it a place of springs; the autumn rains also cover it with pools. They go from strength to strength till each appears before God in Zion.
>
> PSALMS 84:5-7, NIV

I love this verse. It portrays the reality of walking through valleys of pain, grief, and tears. But the psalmist is saying those who have made God their source of strength find their tears are turned into springs of water. As we set our hearts on God, our pain, suffering, and tears are transformed into refreshment and encouragement, not only for ourselves, but also for others. Further, God rains from heaven even more blessings, and they make the springs overflow into pools. Those who continue on their pilgrimage gain more strength day by day until they see God face to face.

We can never doubt this truth if we think about those who have told us about their lives. Corrie ten Boom suffered atrocities in a concentration camp in the 1940s for hiding Jews from the Nazi government, yet God used her to bring many to himself. She was an instrument of God's grace even to those who were her captors.

Joni Eareckson Tada, who nearly thirty years ago suffered a

diving accident and became quadriplegic, has "wheeled" through the valley of tears and made it a spring which has brought glory to God and refreshment to the body of Christ.

I received a call recently from my friend John who lost his wife on Valentine's Day. He called because he said he felt impressed to pray for me. He asked me what chapter I was writing. I told him it was on weeping. He paused for a moment and then said, "I know why I was to call you today. You know, Jan, I've been in such deep despair over losing Tina. But today in my devotional time, it was like I was overcome with joy. As I was reading in the Psalms I couldn't help but be thankful as I saw how faithful God has been over these months. When I read, 'He brought me out into a spacious place; he rescued me because he delighted in me. He makes my feet like the feet of a deer; he enables me to stand on the heights' (Psalms 18:19, 33, NIV), I realized God had truly done that for me. I can hardly believe how God has blessed my business and my personal walk with him. I broke down in tears and wept for joy as I saw the hand of God in my life."

Can you think of a time when you have wept for joy? What surrounded the event? Was it the culmination of a waiting season? Were you able to weep before the Lord with joy?

I experienced a weeping for joy last month. From the time that our daughter Heather was in the womb, I prayed that God would give her a voice to sing praises to him. When Heather was little she used to loved to perform "shows" and would line up her stuffed animal friends on the staircase and perform for her audience. When she reached junior high, she enrolled in the choir at school and seemed to enjoy it.

I saw her interest blooming, but I had no way to evaluate

her talent. Last year her choir teacher pulled me aside and said Heather had a wonderful voice and range for her age. A month ago she started voice lessons. On the way home from her first lesson, Heather turned to me in the car and said with tears in her eyes, "Mom, thank you so much for letting me get voice lessons. I know I'm really going to love it!" I burst into tears of joy. I said, "Oh, Heather, I am so glad we were able to do this for you. Your dad and I have wanted to for a long time. You know this is an answer to prayers I have prayed since before you were born. As I hear you sing so beautifully, it brings such joy to my heart. God has truly answered my prayer."

Throughout a waiting season, there are times for weeping. As you sow your tears in God with a view toward righteousness, breaking up the fallow ground of your heart, you can be assured that one day, you will reap in shouts—even tears—of joy!

Sow with a view to righteousness, reap in accordance with kindness; break up your fallow ground, for it is time to seek the Lord until He comes to rain righteousness on you.

HOSEA 10:12, NASB

EIGHT

When Waiting Brings Willingness

In his book, *A Center of Quiet*, David Runcorn writes, "Having to wait involves a submission. We cannot force the bus to arrive any sooner or the doctor's waiting room to empty faster. But our fury over a train delay or even petty disruptions to our timetable shows how hard we find it to live with the truth of this. Waiting is an acknowledgment of our dependency. It exposes to us the illusion of our 'control' over our lives."[1]

I think of our friend Al, who ten years ago began to pursue his law degree. He and his wife talked extensively about the cost this would exact from their family. He would have to continue to work full-time, as well as go to school. After much prayer, he took the necessary exam, applied to law school, and was accepted. He and his wife viewed these circumstances as doors God had opened. Al had originally attended one year of law school before they married, but dropped out. When it became clear that again the doors were opening, he was sure he'd go through law school, pass the exam, and shift careers. It took a tremendous toll on his family life over the three and a half years of classes and study, but they were convinced God was leading the way.

Shortly before Al was to take the bar exam, his father was

diagnosed with cancer. This, along with other family situations, prohibited Al from taking the exam for four years. During that waiting period, Al struggled to understand God's timing. *Why did we go down this road in the first place? Why did you have me do all this, if I wasn't going to even get the chance to take the exam? Was the sacrifice of time away from my family for nothing?*

Like Al, most of us struggle with waiting. If we have stepped out and done what we believe God has led us to do, we feel cheated or tricked when we don't receive what we think will be secured by our obedience. Americans have been conditioned to expect immediate gratification. We want to see the results in a timely fashion. (Don calls this the "health spa mentality." He is amazed at how many people join their local fitness centers and expect themselves to become fit just because they signed up, in spite of their sporadic workouts.)

We lack in our society, and even in the Christian community, what Eugene Peterson calls "a long obedience in the same direction." In his book by that title, from which I have already quoted, he writes, "Perseverance does not mean 'perfect.' It means we keep going. We do not quit when we find that we are not yet mature and that there is a long journey still before us.... Endurance is not a desperate hanging on, but a traveling from strength to strength."[2]

Al made it through that waiting period and took the bar exam. He failed it.

After considerable prayer, he and his wife decided he should try again, even though they were financially strained. He had already dedicated too much time and energy to stop now. He took the exam again a year later. After finishing the three-day exam, he sat in his car and prayed a prayer of thanks, not knowing whether he had passed, but knowing God had been with him. He found out in November he had failed again. He said there was a moment of disappointment when he asked God, "So what do we do now?"

Al doesn't know if he'll take the bar exam again. Right now, he's willing to wait and trust, even when he can't see the outcome. When we read situations similar to Al's, we immediately begin to wonder if he did the right thing. Was he obedient? Did he really hear God in the beginning? If so, why hasn't it turned out like he'd hoped?

The truth is, we can hear God, be obedient to his call, and still not see the fruit of our labor. That is where faith comes in.

Waiting often brings us to peaceful acceptance, to willingness. Willingness is not a passive resignation, but active trust. We are willing not only to wait, but to examine our motives, to confess our sin, to step out in obedience, and to surrender our rights, in confidence.

What's Your Trust Level?

In the past, if someone had asked me, "Do you trust God?" I would have answered, "Of course I do." But my inner apprehensions spoke louder than words when it came to trusting God with the unknown. I've often felt I have known better than God what is best. I've been unable to rest in God because I've not been sure I could trust him to act on my behalf.

Trust is primary in any relationship. It is vital if we are to move on in our spiritual lives. God was always wanting to bring me to a new level of faith and trust in him. But first, he was going to have to deal squarely with my lack of trust. As I discovered in my dilemma with Kellie's school, my tendency was to run around frantically trying to resolve the dilemma myself, instead of trusting God's goodness and his willingness to intervene.

At the time, I thought God wasn't willing to help fast enough, but now I understand that *the issue was not about God's willingness, but about my own.* By the time my "Now, God!" turned into an "I trust you, Father," my journey home was almost complete.

Oswald Chambers wrote, "Faith, by its very nature must be tried, and the real trial of faith is not that we find it difficult to trust God, but that *God's character has to be cleared in our own minds.*"[3] If we have trouble trusting, obeying, surrendering, or waiting, it probably means we have not settled in our own hearts the truth about God's true character and nature. I am convinced that those of us who desire to move on in God must face the discrepancy between our stated beliefs and the true state of our hearts. Until we do, we will be like a runner who is striving for the finish line while tethered to the starting block.

It reminds me of a woman I met by phone recently. Sherryl and her husband began asking God three years ago about whether they should move their business to another state. After a year or so, it seemed clear that God was directing them to move, so they put their house on the market. Since the Lord had confirmed the move, they assumed they would be gone by the next summer. That summer came, as did the next, and still the house was not sold. At first Sherryl wrestled with the delay; she had given up a job in anticipation of the move. One day in prayer she reached a turning point. She questioned the Lord, and then he seemed to ask her a question in return: *Do you want me to make the decision about when you move or do you want to make it?* It stopped her in her tracks. She realized she needed to trust God rather than make assumptions that seemed logical. She said from that day on, she's learned to live each day trusting God for his perfect timing.

A Lesson In Trust

God gave me a glimpse of his heart one day. One spring afternoon, Don and I had planned to "kidnap" our girls from school and surprise them with a trip to nearby Disneyland. It just so happened that the day we had planned our trip, Kellie's class was having a special party for one of her teacher's aides. They had planned the party for weeks and had worked hard to keep it a secret. I saw how excited Kellie was about it. Don and I discussed everything, but we decided to proceed with our secret plan. I did tell Kellie the day of the party that I would be picking her up early. She looked puzzled.

"What's going on, Mom? You know today is my party."

"Honey, I know it is and I know you've been looking forward to it. But if you will just trust me, I promise you won't be disappointed. I can't tell you what this is about, but I think you'll like what has been planned."

Kellie was still a bit confused but she was willing to go along with the unknown plan. Later that afternoon, we picked up both girls at school. We were off. As we drove a different route to the amusement park, the girls were not sure what was up. When we turned the corner where the Disneyland sign was in sight, they both began to squeal.

"We're going to Disneyland!" they both cried. "This is great! This is worth missing the party!"

About a week later, I wrote the following in my journal:

Lord, there's such a war within me. I guess I feel inside that yielding and surrendering usually leads to disappointment and loss, and so I hang on desperately and continue to struggle for my own solutions to prevail.

Come, child. There has been no one in your life who has consistently demonstrated my kind of love. For that reason you have found the need to fend for yourself. Come child, rest awhile in my arms. I have no ulterior motive. I have all that your heart has longed for.

Lord, I struggle with yielding and surrendering my will and desires. I realize how much bitterness I have held in my heart toward you when I have been disappointed. Please forgive me. I'm not sure I really know how to "let go" in such a way that I am not bothered by the outcome. Oh, Lord, help my unbelief, my lack of faith and trust....

Jan, don't you see my heart for you? Last Friday with your girls, you had a bigger, better plan than they knew.

Kellie, especially, had to be *willing to trust you*—to give up a special party at school to go to an unknown place. Because she trusts your love for her, she could let go of her expectation and look excitedly toward the unknown. If she had only focused on what she would miss, she would have missed the blessing of the special trip. Letting go means that you trust in the depths of your heart that I do love you and want to bring blessing and good things into your life. I am your Father who loves you, who has your best interest at heart. I delight to bring you good things and to bless you with joys unspeakable. *I love you both by the things I give and the things I withhold.*

I knew God was calling me to trust him beyond what I could see. Could I trust God as Kellie had trusted me? Could I let go of trying to work it out myself? Could I trust God's plan if he did not change things? I knew I *should* trust him, but was I *willing*?

When I was a child, every birthday card I received from my grandparents included a couple of dollars and my grandparents' signature, under which my grandmother always wrote the Scripture, "Trust in the Lord with all your heart, and lean not on your own understanding. In all your ways acknowledge Him, and He shall direct your paths" (Proverbs 3:5-6, NKJV). I've had to rehearse those words, admonishing myself not to lean on my own understanding. He has always been calling me to trust him.

You may be at a crossroads in your own life. You have exhausted all your efforts to try to work out the dilemma, but it still remains. The questions that may torment you are not easily answered:

- Is it time to move on or stay where we are?

- Is God going to heal my child or is this an illness we will have to learn to accept?

- Am I destined to be single or will the right person ever come along?

- Is the job I've been praying for around the corner or is it not in God's will?

- Will my relationship with my husband ever have the intimacy I long for or am I to live out this marriage in isolation?

Whatever your question may be, are you willing to trust God with it? Your willingness to trust is the first step. After that, God's Spirit may lead you to a willingness to look at your motives before you can move on to obedience or surrender.

What Are Your Motives?

David Runcorn writes, "Waiting sharpens desire. In fact it helps us to recognize where our real desires lie. It separates our passing enthusiasms from our true longings. It reveals to us both our shallowness and our depths. Waiting is a test of our love and longing."[4]

Have you found this to be true for you? I certainly have. Waiting has a way of shifting and sifting us. Sometimes the sifting makes us face ourselves more honestly, exposing our true motives. In James 4:3 we're told that we ask but do not receive, because we ask with wrong motives.

A few years ago I wanted to sell our house. I wanted to have a larger home for our girls when they reached adolescence. We put our home up for sale two years in a row and nothing happened. The third year we were planning to put it up for sale, God started dealing with me about my motives. It was true that I desired to have a larger home so we could have Bible studies, church activities, and room for our daughters' friends in our home, but I had another hidden reason. Every holiday, Don's family functions were over at my sister-in-law's house. Frankly, I was jealous. I wanted a bigger, better house than she had so the family would come to *my* home. I was jealous because it seemed to me that my mother-in-law liked her a whole lot better than she did me. As we put our house on the market for the third year in a row, I felt impressed by the Lord to confess my selfish motives and I asked him to cleanse me and purify my heart. In turn, I felt he was asking me to go to my sister-in-law to confess my jealousy, which she knew nothing about.

I could not escape the conviction of the Holy Spirit and found myself at her front door, asking if I could speak to her alone. We went to their study, which transformed itself into a confessional when she opened the door. I confessed my jealousy and asked for her forgiveness. She was very gracious and we cleared the air on some other unresolved issues. I left knowing I had done the right thing. Our house sold within a month after I met with my sister-in-law.

As most of us realize, our houses won't always sell, even if we do confess our sins; our obedience doesn't always secure immediate resolution or guarantee a long-awaited answer to prayers. Our obedience evidences our love for the One whom we trust. In his book, *After the Spirit Comes,* Jack Taylor wrote, "We may not understand the proceedings, but then, we are not called to understand.... only to obey.... God will go to almost any extreme to get us in circumstances so as to discover that part of our ego yet uncrucified and expose it to the killing rays of Calvary...."[5]

As we're called upon to wait in life, we are challenged to re-evaluate our goals, dissect our dreams, and purify our motives. Waiting brings about winnowing as we are continually in the process of being conformed to the image of Christ and being "transformed into his likeness" (2 Corinthians 3:18, NIV).

Consider the idea that God may be calling you to examine your motives or reevaluate your goals. What are the motives behind your desires? Are you willing to allow God to readjust your desires to coincide with his will for your life? Tell him you are willing. You may find, as I did, you need to enter into the next step which is a willingness to confess your sin.

Confession is Good for the Soul

Some of you looked at this section and were about to skip it because confession is not something you look forward to. I couldn't agree with you more. I love others to exercise their confession muscle with regard to me, but I feel embarrassed to show others my pitiful muscle in public. I'd much rather keep it a matter between me and the Lord.

I realized some years ago that some of my most spiritual requests could not be advanced until I was willing to confess my sin. Psalm 66 is quite blunt about it: if I "regard iniquity in my heart, the Lord will not hear" (v. 18, NKJV).

Sometimes we harbor sin in our hearts. Other times, it amounts to "unfinished business" with God. We may need to acknowledge our sin or seek reconciliation with another person. Still other times, God seems simply to want us to confess. Confession often deepens intimacy. I've known several couples who have entered marriage counseling because they desire a closer relationship or better communication skills. As the couple's counseling proceeds, one may confess a wrong response or attitude to the other. Basic willingness to humbly confess not only clears the offense, but also brings them into a deeper, more intimate relationship.

When I was in graduate school at a Christian university, I had a problem with pride. I was deeply convicted. I genuinely sought the Lord and asked him to deal with the pride in my life. Have you ever prayed a prayer like that? Watch out! He will take you at your word.

I forgot about the prayer and life went on. One evening in one of my classes, I was relating a story to the entire class of thirty-eight students and my two professors. As I was telling the story, I lied to embellish the story and make it a bit more interesting. After class, while driving home, I felt the conviction of the Holy Spirit. I confessed immediately, agreeing with God that I had lied and that I knew what I was doing when I chose to relate the story as I did.

The next day in my devotional time, the Spirit seemed to say, "When you go back to class next Monday, you need to confess to the class publicly that you lied and ask for their forgiveness." I immediately dismissed this thought—this was out of the question! Two days went by and the conviction became heavier. I tried rationalizing with the Lord. *Lord, can't we just keep this between you and me? They will never find out that I lied. Besides that, they all know I am a Christian speaker and it will ruin my reputation of integrity.* He then reminded me of my prayer. I couldn't bear the thought of confessing to my classmates. *Can't we deal with my pride some other way, Lord?*

The Sunday before I was to return to class on Monday, I had been wrestling with it for days and could not even tell my husband what I had done. Sunday afternoon Don went to the hardware store to pick up a light switch and some other items. When he came in the door he said, "Honey, you are going to be so proud of me."

I said, "I am? How come?"

"Well, you know, I went to the hardware store. When I was halfway home, I looked down at the receipt and realized the clerk had given me back too much money. Then I thought of you. I thought about how many times you have been such an example of integrity and honesty concerning things like this, so I turned the car around and went back to the store to give the money back. I said to myself, *if Jan were in this situation, I know this is what she would do because she's such a woman of integrity.*"

"Thank you so much for sharing that with me," I said to Don sheepishly. He looked a little puzzled by my response, so I told him about what I had done in class the previous week. Now I know that God has a sense of humor. Why else would he go to the trouble to send Don to the hardware store twice to get his poor prideful wife's attention? I asked Don to pray for me.

The next day, having rehearsed my confession throughout the short night, I was sitting in class, much quieter than normal. Near the end of the four-hour session, the man sitting next to me looked over at me and said, "Jan, you don't look very good, are you feeling OK?" Even thinking about confessing was making me look sick.

I could wait no longer. I raised my flimsy little arm and was called on by one of the professors. The tears started flowing soon after I got out my first few words. I shared how I had asked the Lord to deal with my pride and then proceeded to tell the class how I had lied. I asked for their forgiveness. There was a hush over the room. All eyes were riveted on me. I thought I would melt, but I made it through.

After class was over, several of my classmates came up to me and thanked me, telling me how they appreciated my confession and how much courage it took to do that. Others were saying how spiritual I was to be obedient to something as difficult as this was. As they were speaking, thoughts began flashing through my head: *this did take a lot of courage, didn't it?; this was certainly very spiritual of me, wasn't it?; I'm probably one of the most....*

"Wait a minute," I said aloud to those who were standing around affirming me. "I need to confess something to you all right now. Pride is so insidious in my life, I am even taking pride in what you all are telling me right now!" I thought of James 5:16, which reads, "Therefore, confess your sins to one another, and pray for one another, so that you may be healed" (NASB).

I wish I could tell you that I have never had to deal with pride again! That could not be farther from the truth, but I know that my willingness to confess brings me into right relationship with the One who bore my shame and who has the ability to set me free from "the sin that so easily entangles" (Hebrews 12:1, NIV).

Think about the waiting season you are in. Is it a matter of being willing to trust, to examine your motives, or to confess your sin? God is waiting that he might be gracious to you. Don't *you* wait any longer. Confess whatever it is that is holding you back at the starting block. Determine to step out in obedience today.

Willingness to Step Out

Nehemiah is a good example of one who was willing to step out in obedience. The historical background is crucial to the understanding of what Nehemiah did. The Jewish people had been exiled for seventy years in Babylon, returning to Judea in 536 B.C., just as God had promised. Upon their return to Jerusalem, they committed themselves to rebuilding the temple, which took them twenty years. It was now seventy years since the completion of the temple and Nehemiah was questioning some visitors from Judah, asking about the remnant who had survived the exile and about the state of Jerusalem. They reported to him, "Those who survived the exile and are back in the province are in great trouble and disgrace. The wall of Jerusalem is broken down, and its gates have been burned with fire." When Nehemiah heard these things he sat down and wept (Nehemiah 1:3-4, NIV). In his grief, Nehemiah also set himself to fasting and prayer. It was good to have rebuilt the temple, but a city with no walls remained both vulnerable and incomplete. In fact, as God's holy city, it was considered a reproach to God.

Nehemiah prayed and sought the Lord for four months without mentioning a word to anyone. The day came for him to step out. The scene is recorded in Scripture:

> I took the wine and gave it to the king. I had not been sad in his presence before; so the king asked me, "Why does your face look so sad when you are not ill? This can be nothing but sadness of heart." I was very much afraid, but I said to the king, "May the king live forever! Why should my face not look sad when the city where my fathers are buried lies in ruins, and its gates have been destroyed by fire?"
>
> NEHEMIAH 2:1b-3

Why, you may be asking, was he so afraid to be honest? In ancient times, no one was to enter the presence of the king without "radiating a sense of privilege," and violating this accepted protocol could have resulted in removal from one's position, banishment, or death. Nehemiah risked his own security and prestige out of his intense concern for his people and Jerusalem.[6]

King Artaxerxes immediately asked what it was that Nehemiah wanted. Nehemiah "prayed to the God of heaven" and proceeded to ask that he might be allowed to go to

Jerusalem to rebuild the city walls. Nehemiah gave a detailed account of all that he needed to complete the project, including a time estimate. He had waited patiently before the Lord, but was anything but idle during that time. He was planning, preparing, estimating, and evaluating. When the king gave the OK, he was ready for action.

This is wise as well as courageous. Most of us hesitate to step out at least sometimes. When you have difficulty stepping out, you may need to be willing to take some initial steps toward preparation. What might some of these preparatory steps be?

1. Pray. Complacent people forget to pray for change because they see no need for it. If this is you, make a regular commitment at least every six months to spend a week seeking God about whether he desires any changes in your life or circumstances. "Pray about everything..." (Philippians 4:6, LB).

2. Pay attention to circumstantial indicators. God sometimes uses our circumstances to nudge us out of complacency. In his book, *How to Listen to God,* Charles Stanley wrote, "God knows exactly what it takes to get our attention, and often it is through highly unusual circumstances that we stand back and take note of what God is doing in our lives."[7] If you are in a difficult work situation, God *may* allow it to worsen, to get your attention. Always take the circumstantial indicators to God in prayer. Also, seek counsel from a wise friend or spiritual mentor.

3. Prepare for possible changes. About five years ago, I asked Don if he had any desire to pursue an administrative credential which would allow him to become a principal in his school district. At the time, he said he was quite satisfied and really could not see himself in the role of an administrator. Six months ago, Don came to me and said he was thinking about getting his credential. He'd given it some thought over the past year, especially since he wasn't sure how much longer he could coach, and he was looking ahead to retirement. For him, this is a stepping-out. He is willing to pursue a new avenue, *not* what he has always dreamed of, in order to provide for our family.

4. Purpose to follow God. This is probably the most important of all for those who have apprehensions about stepping out. It may mean you will be taken from your comfort zone, but the rewards far outweigh the temporary fears and hardships. Such decisiveness is an active response to a challenging situation.

Nehemiah was one who encountered many obstacles during the rebuilding process, but over and over in the Scripture, he acknowledged that "the good hand of my God was on me" (Nehemiah 2:8, NASB). He didn't let the obstacles deter him from continuing to pursue the vision.

I have talked to many men and women who, in the winter of their lives, lament over what they wish they had accomplished. I rarely hear them say they regret having stepped out in faith. On the contrary, they wish they had stepped out more often.

It may be that God is asking you to take the first step. I think again of Peter, whose impetuous nature is often portrayed as a weakness. Do you realize there were eleven other disciples in the boat the day Jesus walked on the water? (See Matthew 14:24-33.) Only one man, Peter, actually took the step out of the boat and walked on the water toward Jesus. Will you purpose to do the same?

Willingness to Surrender

To me, "surrender" had always been equated with "giving up." "Giving up" meant "no change" or "losing out." I had learned it when I was young. When my dad had been rigid or abusive, my mother would say, "That's just the way your dad is; you're not going to change him, so you'll have to adjust."

All my life, acquiescence to futility, relabeled "acceptance," had always been detestable to me. Anytime I heard someone say, "It can't be done," my immediate response was, "Watch me." I took great pride in fighting against the odds. I didn't respect those who "gave up" because life was too hard, and I'd made a vow never to accept what could be changed. As a result, I resisted God's every attempt to bring me to the place of surrender. To me, surrender meant forsaking the needs of one who is weak, to accommodate and appease one who is already strong.

According to the dictionary, surrender means to "yield to the power or control of another." To do so without reservation, we must be assured that our vulnerability will not be exploited. We must have a level of security, safety, love, and trust. Even though the Lord had certainly demonstrated his kind of tenderness in my life, I found myself holding in reserve certain areas which I could not surrender to him because of fear. One of those was my children.

To surrender my second-grader to the school system, trusting only in the Lord's protection, seemed tantamount to throwing her to the lions. I felt undue anguish at the prospect. In fact, I was mad at God:

Lord, this isn't a good situation for Kellie, and yet there seems to be no hope for resolution. I feel that I can't depend on you, Lord, to work these things out, so I must step in. Why do you wait? She is just a little girl! How can you make her bear these hurts? I am mad at you for leaving me in this state— for having me carry all of this alone. There is no one to save, no one to help.

I had reached a dead end. Even though I thought I might be able to exert enough pressure to get Kellie's classroom changed, I knew inside God was asking me to surrender the situation to him. It was doubly difficult because I was flipping back and forth between the helplessness I felt now as a mother and the abandonment I had felt before, as a child.

A.W. Tozer wrote, "We are often hindered from giving up our treasures to the Lord out of fear for their safety; this is especially true when those treasures are loved relatives and friends. But we need have no such fears. Our Lord came not to destroy but to save. Everything is safe which we commit to Him and nothing is really safe which is not so committed."[8] I knew God was calling me to entrust my child to him. Through surrendering this situation into his hands, I was taking a step in that direction.

For me to surrender my child seemed as though I were abandoning her, leaving her as open prey. But the Lord was showing me that surrendering Kellie was like returning to the good Shepherd one of his little lambs, which had inadvertently been caught in a thicket and was in need of his special care and attention. Because of his love for me and my love for the little lamb, he would draw me in as well, teaching me how best to comfort and soothe her injuries. Through this experience, both the little lamb and I would forever be bonded in love to the only One who binds up broken hearts and sets captives free. He is the Good Shepherd.

So I did it, finally. I will never forget that day. As I lifted my hands symbolically surrendering Kellie and the entire situation to him, I saw no lightning bolts. I heard no promises. I can't even say it was a "peaceful letting go in strength and confidence." It was a simple act of agony. I felt ripped up inside. But I knew my Shepherd understood. I knew he was there to comfort this little lamb, and in turn, I was to pass on that comfort to Kellie.

Waiting had brought me to the place of being willing to trust God with my child and finally to the place of surrender. As I've waited in and through other situations, I've had to learn to be willing to examine my motives, confess my sin, and step out in obedience.

I spoke with our friend Al today. He still has not passed the bar, and his career is in "limbo." He's come to a similar place. I asked what he has learned about waiting. He paused, then said, "I know now that it doesn't have to turn out the way I wanted. I've come to a stronger sense that God is in control."

The Lord may be tugging at your heart. Is there a barrier

that keeps you from fully trusting him? As you are willing, he will help to remove it. Do you recognize your need to examine your motives? Can you be honest with yourself and God about them? Once you have, you may need to be willing to confess. He promises that he will not turn away from those who are of a broken and contrite heart (see Psalm 51:17, NIV). Perhaps you are one who needs the willingness to step out. Ask the Lord to strengthen your feeble knees and to give you the courage to step out of the boat. Remember that the nature of God's redemptive work is that of surrender—he will not force you.

Many have traveled this way before us. A.W. Tozer wrote: "The man that has the most of God is the man who is seeking the most ardently for more of God."[9]

A willingness to surrender and make peace with God and others promises to yield a "harvest of righteousness" (James 3:18, NIV).

PART THREE

Harvest Home

NINE

When Waiting Becomes Wisdom

I sat at a table with wisdom recently. I was a keynote speaker in Calgary, Alberta, Canada, along with a gentleman whom I had never met. When I first was introduced to Dr. David Schroeder, I remember thinking how gentle and mild-mannered he was. He has been a theology professor for over forty years at a small Mennonite college in Canada. At seventy-two years of age, he is bright, articulate, and witty. As I listened to his teaching for three days, I marveled at his simplicity and wisdom. Over each of the meals we shared with the conference organizers, I found myself pursuing him with questions.

Around the table with ten others, I asked what he had learned about waiting. With a gentle smile, he shared how twenty years ago he had returned to the seminary which he had attended as a young man. He went to visit the wife of the seminary president, who was now quite aged and living in a rest home. When she had seen him, she had remarked, "David, I'm so happy to see that you have become more patient over these years." He chuckled a bit. They had reflected together about how impatient he had been as a young seminary student. He looked at me and simply said, "I suppose I have learned to be more patient."

The night before we were to leave for our respective homes, I asked Dr. Schroeder if he would allow me to ask him a few questions. We sat together in the lobby of the hotel. As I formulated my first question, tears welled up in my eyes. I'm not sure Dr. Schroeder knew why, but I did. I realized how very much I missed my wise Grandpa Mitchell, and my Grandma Garrett, both of whom were godly influences in my early life. Oh, how I had wished they were still living so I might ask them the deep spiritual questions that often weighed on my heart.

A bit tearfully, I asked, "If I were your daughter and asked you for one bit of advice that would guide me in my spiritual walk, what would it be?"

He paused for a moment. Then he said, "Don't come to God with loaded expectations."

We sat for awhile longer as he shared with me about his life. As a young man he was convinced he was to be in the pastorate, but at the age of twenty-nine he contracted polio, which changed his life's direction.

"When I am not sure which way I am to go, I look for the promise of life and the promise of God. I look for whatever seems to be the direction which promises the most life for others around me. When I find that, I follow it with all my heart. If it truly is the direction of God, it will be accompanied by signs of fulfillment. There will be an evidence of fruit. If there is not, then I know I have made a mistake."

I interjected, "What do you do when you discover you've made a mistake?"

"I repent before the Lord and go on doing what I know to do," he said genuinely.

We parted that evening. The following morning before dawn we shared a taxi to the airport. Every contact with him had been a privilege. I doubt Dr. Schroeder knows the impact of his humility and wisdom on others. I guess that is the very nature of humility and wisdom—they are unaware of their inviting, persuasive presence.

I thought about wisdom and its connection to waiting. What is wisdom? Carole Mayhall has written: "A prerequisite of wisdom is knowledge. One has to know about something (knowledge) before one can take a proper course of action (wisdom)."[1] It is the knowledge we gain through waiting that becomes a harvest of wisdom as we faithfully apply it in future circumstances.

This makes me wonder what I have learned. Has my knowledge increased as a result of waiting? Have I in fact gained wisdom along the way?

These questions can only be answered as I remember where I am now compared to where I was. Most of us start out on an unknown journey. Later, we begin to understand where we have traveled and what we have learned.

An Unknown Journey

When I began journaling my prayers, I had no idea that God was going to use my journal entries as a means of teaching me about the journey of waiting. As I made my original entries I did not choose my words. I was merely a sojourner in the desert of waiting trying to find God's direction in the midst of a fog. But God was at work in me to accomplish his purpose, long before I knew what that purpose was. I wrote:

Lord, it seems as though you only show me a small portion of your plan at a time. Am I unable to handle more? Are you trying to teach me a closer walk? Even as I ask this, I know what the answer is. I am like a person on a journey who asks for directions but who doesn't depend on them anyway. You are only giving me a few steps and turns at a time, requiring me to be ever aware of my need for you. Is the final destination any less certain? Of course it is not, but my heart often feels uncertain. How accustomed I must become to your larger view!

I learned from Oswald Chambers:

There are times in spiritual life when there is confusion, and it is no way out to say that there ought not to be confusion. It is not a question of right and wrong, but a question of God taking you by a way which in the meantime you do not understand, and it is only by going through the confusion that you will get at what God wants.... Jesus says there are times when your Father will appear as if He were an unnatural father, as if He were callous and indifferent, but remember He is not;... If there is a shadow on the face of the Father just now, hang onto it that He will ultimately give His clear revealing and justify Himself in all that He permitted.[2]

I also learned from a real-life experience. We had planned for years to take our daughters on an East Coast adventure.

Don, who majored in history, has always encouraged our girls' interest in historical facts, geography, and trivia. The girls were finally old enough to benefit from experiencing all the historical sites in Washington D.C., Williamsburg, Boston, Philadelphia, Gettysburg, and New York City. Don is a wonder when it comes to planning our vacations. He spends hours preparing our itinerary, mapping out our route, securing our accommodations, and reading biographies or other travel books to prepare himself to be our well-informed travel guide.

Don had told us from the outset that the longest drive of our trip would be the one from Cooperstown, New York, to Lexington, Kentucky. He estimated it would take thirteen hours, but he planned to leave before dawn, so we could sleep while he drove.

What Don did not know was that we were to encounter major fog the morning of our departure. As we got into the car, Don asked me to help navigate him toward the highway, after which I would be free to sleep while he drove. We managed to get on the highway, but the fog was so dense we could barely see ten feet in front of us. I was very tense and nervous. I was afraid that Don would plow into an unseen vehicle or miss our intended turnoff. Outside the window was nothing but the blanket of fog in the dark. I went into a hyper-vigilant mode. *Stay alert. Watch the road. Make sure Don stays awake!* Don tried to reassure me, but nothing seemed to ease my anxiety. He encouraged me to try to sleep, but there was no way I was going to let him navigate on his own in those conditions.

Before long, I heard the Spirit of God whispering to my

heart. He was comparing this fog to what I was experiencing in my spiritual life at present. I was anxious and fearful because the road ahead was not clearly visible. God was not lifting the fog in my life, but was asking me to follow him without being able to see exactly where I was going. He was attempting to comfort me and assure me that all would be well, and that together we would reach the destination he had planned. He then clearly told me to trust my husband, lean back in the seat, and rest in his ability to bring us through the fog. It was against my natural reactions to relinquish my tension, but I did so. To my surprise, I fell asleep. When I awoke two hours later, the fog had lifted, the highway had cleared, and we were well on our way to Lexington.

I must confess, I still ask God to let me in on what he has planned, but I know that if he were to always do that, I would never grow in faith. He does allow us to go through seasons when we *feel* he has withdrawn or his direction seems obscured. These seasons are ultimately for our growth and good, teaching us to live by faith and not by sight alone.

I can now look back and see some of what God was trying to teach me, but in the midst of the lesson, I could only see a short distance ahead. I think that is the nature of walking with God. There is no set formula to follow. Sometimes he gives us explicit instructions as to our direction and purpose. He did that for Moses (see Exodus 3:10). Other times, he shows us only one step and then asks us to wait, as he did with Paul at his conversion (see Acts 9:5-9).

It is helpful for all of us to review how God has led us in the past so that, as we remember, our faith is built up and we can face the future with hope.

Remember Our Journey

Remembering the journey is an important part of gaining wisdom. Spurgeon wrote: "Forget not what thy God has done for thee; turn over the book of thy remembrance, and consider the days of old.... Go back then, a little way to the choice mercies of yesterday, and though all may be dark now, light up the lamps of the past, they shall glitter through the darkness and thou shalt trust in the Lord till the day break and the shadows flee away."[3]

God's Spirit reminds me about the manna he provided the Israelites in the wilderness. He says, "Yesterday's manna is not meant to be your provision for today—it is to be brought to remembrance to bring you hope."

Reflect on different struggles, past prayer requests, previous waiting seasons which you have weathered or had answered, and take note of the lessons you have learned. You will be encouraged to remain faithful.

Moses specifically instructed the Israelites to *remember:*

Remember how the Lord your God led you all the way in the desert these forty years, to humble you and to test you in order to know what was in your heart, whether or not you would keep his commands.   DEUTERONOMY 8:2, NIV

Moses admonishes the people not to forget all that the Lord has done for them. He reminds them of the way God brought them out of the slavery of Egypt, through the vast desert, provided water from a rock, and manna from heaven, to humble them and test them, "so that in the end it might go well with them" (Deuteronomy 8:16, NIV). I am thankful that God saw fit to encourage the chronicling of Israel's journey; "these things happened to them as an example, and they were written for our instruction" (1 Corinthians 10:11, NASB).

Here's an exercise: sit down with a piece of paper and draw a line down the center. On the left side, write down as many past incidents, struggles, or prayer requests you faced that are no longer unresolved. On the right side, briefly describe how that situation was resolved, or how you've come to peace with it in your own heart. Examine each one carefully and look at what you may have learned as a result. Take note of any ways you can now see God's hand. Now take time to praise and thank him for his faithfulness. The grace which was at work then is still working in your life today. "Jesus Christ is the same yesterday and today and forever"(Hebrews 13:8, NIV).

Recording the lessons we have learned helps us to appropriate the knowledge for future situations. This is the meaning of wisdom.

Record the Lessons Learned

As a parent, as I have had to remind my daughters, repeatedly, of lessons I think they should have learned by now. After lecturing my teen for the umpteenth time about being responsible, I've asked myself, *When is she going to learn this lesson?*

Then I catch myself and realize God is probably wondering

the same thing about me! So often I am like the Israelites. When will a lesson learned in one situation begin to be easier to recall for the next time? Perhaps that is why God required Israel to make "pillars of remembrance" in the Old Testament. They were tangible memorials commemorating a demonstration of God's faithfulness, meant to be a visible reminder of past predicaments and God's dependable provision.

The Lord told Joshua to appoint twelve men, one from each of the twelve tribes, to take up a stone with them as they passed over the Jordan. The stones were to serve as a "sign," "a memorial to the people of Israel forever" (Joshua 4:7, NIV). Further,

> Joshua said to the Israelites: "In the future, when your descendants ask their fathers 'What do these stones mean?' tell them, 'Israel crossed the Jordan on dry ground. For the Lord your God dried up the Jordan before you until you had crossed over. The Lord your God did to the Jordan just what he had done to the Red Sea when he dried it up before us until we had crossed over. He did this so that all the peoples of the earth might know that the hand of the LORD is powerful and so that you might always fear the Lord your God.'"   JOSHUA 4:21-24, NIV

What do we see here? Joshua had learned the lesson— "God will make a way where there is no way." He was one of the two remaining Israelites who had witnessed the parting of the Red Sea. He was recalling to them his own journey, lest it be forgotten.

Our own pillars of remembrance may not be piles of river stones, and they may not be recorded for all posterity, but they not only serve to remind us of what we've learned, they also serve as testimonies to those around us.

What helps you to preserve cherished family memories? Don is our official photo album organizer. Each year, he puts together a photo album centered around a particular theme descriptive of our summer vacation. Over the years we've had such themes as: "Side by Side," "Heat Wave," "Team Player," "Dancin' in the Streets," and "Passport to Adventure." Our friends are amazed at the wonderful product Don creates each year. We often sit down as a family to reminisce about the highlights of a trip and enjoy reading Don's captions, which help remind us of special moments.

Have you considered doing the same in your relationship with God? Can you create an "album" which commemorates answers to prayer or lessons you have learned in your spiritual life? Have you passed on a godly legacy of remembrance to your children?

Notice I did not say "an album which commemorates perfection"! If we waited to put together a commemorative journal of our final successes, most of us would never do one. However, we do need to record our progress so that we can be encouraged and be of comfort to other pilgrims along the way. Even Paul, writing to Timothy, urged, "Be diligent in these matters; give yourself wholly to them, so that everyone may see your progress" (1 Timothy 4:15, NIV). For me, journaling my prayers has been one of the richest ways I have found of marking my spiritual journey. It has provided me with insight, encouragement, and wisdom as I've seen the tender way in which the Lord has guided me and ministered to the deepest needs of my heart.

What lessons have you learned over the recent months as you've walked with God? Have you learned some insights during a waiting season? Have you commemorated or recorded the ways he has been faithful to you along the way? If not, begin today. As you remember your journey and record the lessons, you are building pillars of remembrance that may encourage future generations.

Lessons from the Garden

As I wrote earlier, some of the most profound lessons I have learned about waiting have come through my daughter Kellie's garden. I know now it was no coincidence that Kellie obtained access to her plot of ground during the writing of this book. As I've watched her, I've learned something of the heart of God. I asked her not too long ago what it is that she enjoys so much about her garden. She said, "Mom, I love watching things grow and seeing how they turn out."

I expressed my own observation of the hard work that's involved and then asked what it was that brought her so much satisfaction. She said, "When I go out to the garden, I see in my mind how it is going to look. I feel good knowing I've provided something for our family to eat. When I planted those strawberry plants the other day, I didn't think about how much time it took me, I just thought about all the strawberries we'll have."

These were treasures of wisdom coming from my twelve-year-old. How many times have I been discouraged and disillusioned as I have had to wait through a hardship or trial, wanting to give up or give in. I didn't bother to look at what God was trying to produce in the garden of my heart through difficult times. Kellie helped me to see what it must be like from God's perspective. He takes joy and delight from what he sees will be the harvest of his planting. He doesn't get caught up in all the circumstantial trivialities.

I couldn't resist questioning my daughter further. "Kellie, how do you feel about the fact that your carrots didn't do very well? Are you disappointed they didn't grow as well as you'd hoped?" She immediately responded, "Mom, this isn't the *only* time I'm going to plant carrots. I've learned not to use seed tape, and I've learned some other things that will help me the next time."

I was impressed. I myself would admit failure with carrots and never plant another one again. She, on the other hand, was using her experience as a means of learning and growth. *Lord, how many times I've run from my failures rather than gleaning and incorporating important truths that would help me to grow....*

What wisdom have I gleaned in my waiting seasons? I have caught a greater glimpse of God's love, his vast sovereignty, his tender-hearted response to my questions and longings. I look into my journals and see how God was at work to bring a harvest from a time in my life which seemed barren and fruitless. I have come to the place of rest, knowing in the depths of my heart the goodness of God. I have not yet learned enough, but I am learning to trust God and his timetable. I'm learning to adjust my perspective; to glance at the temporal and gaze upon the eternal. I'm learning to rely on his faithfulness—and to rest.

Learning to Rest

Early in the waiting season, I knew God was wanting to teach me about entering into his rest. I was familiar with the Scriptures that spoke of God's rest and the section in the fourth chapter of the letter to the Hebrews which talked about Israel's inability to enter into God's rest because of unbelief. I detailed part of my struggle:

Lord, this not knowing and the constant wondering create such an unsettled place in my heart. I know you are trying to teach me to rest in you—to be anchored in you. All my unknowns are not unknown to you. Let me rest in the knowledge that you have a plan and that you will reveal what I need to know when the time is right.

I do think of my own children, Lord. How anxious they become when they want certain things and don't realize that I share their desires. They become impatient, insistent, and want to push their desires into existence. I know that I do that with you at times. I do delight to give my girls things that delight their hearts. Do you have those same desires toward me, Lord? Do you long to teach me a deeper love than that which is communicated by the giving of material things?

I am realizing how necessary it is to be quiet and still in order to receive such a love. Forgive me, Lord, for rushing off and refusing to rest. Isaiah 30:15 is truly what you have called me to: "In repentance [coming home to the Father] and rest you shall be saved, in quietness and trust is your strength" (NASB).

One day as I prayed, the Lord brought to mind the following scene: I was sitting in my favorite love seat with pillows cushioning my back and my feet propped up. Both my children ran up to me asking, "What do I do now, Mommy?" Each would run away after I gave them some instruction, but be back in a flash to ask frantically, "Now what?" "What next, Mom?" This repeated itself over and over. Then the Lord stopped me with a question. He said, "How would you feel if this was the extent of your relationship with your girls?" I said, *Oh Lord, I would feel sad if that was all there was to our relationship. I would not want my girls to be so consumed with duties, but I would want them to climb up into my lap so I could love them, share my heart with them, and listen as they shared their hearts with me.*

The parallel to my own pattern with my heavenly Father was obvious. I had become just like my prayer vision. I had been so obsessed with finding out what God's plan was that I'd begun to miss out on the true essence of relationship with him.

Perhaps you are still grappling with the purpose of your waiting season. Perhaps you are too close to the details to see what God was doing or even to sense his presence. "The truth is that the closer we are to someone the less we see of them. Presence becomes more important than sight. Consider a mountain. We see it clearly ahead of us and decide to climb it. But when we start to climb we lose sight of it. It is too close to see.... [But] we press on...."[4] This is an integral part of true wisdom.

Waiting has given me a gift—wisdom. Wisdom has been deepened and broadened through remembering my journey and recording the insights I've learned. I am learning that I can rest in God's faithful care.

Moses prayed, "So teach us to number our days, that we may present to Thee a heart of wisdom" (Psalms 90:12, NASB). Make that your prayer today!

TEN

When Waiting Becomes Wellsprings

In my waiting seasons, I have tended to lose my joy. Sometimes it was missing for quite some time before I noticed, I was so busy "doing." I mistakenly substituted performance for God for presence with God. It was the very quiet of the waiting that revealed the absence of intimacy with God:

Lord, I have so lacked spiritual discipline and I've missed my times with you—forgive me for wandering. You are my first love. I miss you and your Word.... There is no joy without you.

Waiting always helps me refocus my passions and deepen my pursuit of God. I have discovered that the greatest joy is to be found in his presence, not in the resolution to a problem, the answer to a long-awaited prayer, or the end of a waiting season. This is true: "Thou wilt make known to me the path of life; in Thy presence is fulness of joy; in Thy right hand there are pleasures forever" (Psalms 16:11, KJV).

I hope it is clear to you by now that our wondering, wandering, whining, wallowing, wrestling, and weeping are necessary parts of waiting in the presence of God. *Only by going through these stages can we move from the external, to the inter-*

nal, and finally to the eternal focus on God. Most of us would rather arrive at the reward without having to walk the painful path through the desert of discontent. We want to learn to wait—*quickly*—so we need not wait any longer!

"Lord, give me patience—NOW!" There is no quick way to learn patience, unfortunately. And there is nothing romantic about learning simplicity and waiting. It is tough. It involves an emptying. It means a space must be cleared in the midst of the clutter of our lives. And there we must sit and be still and wait for God in hope and patience. It will feel rather useless or a "waste of time." But it is actually challenging our whole understanding of what is useful. This quiet, unhurried work of the Spirit begins when we give space for God at the heart of our lives. It is a silence of humble submission.[1]

Waiting in his presence has helped me to reexamine my relationship with God. I see the many distortions and misconceptions I still hold onto. I have realized that although I've been a Christian for over thirty years, I have been *childish* in my responses to God and what he had allowed in my life. His desire was that I grow up and mature in him.

The irony is that when we grow up in him we become more *child-like*—more dependent, trusting, vulnerable, and honest without reserve. We get beyond our need to have God continually demonstrate his love through phenomenal prayer-answers. We learn to let him be our *Lord,* the one in full charge.

In the middle of my transition from childish faith to maturity, I was surprised by my own discovery about loving God as reflected in my journal:

What good is love if you don't feel it? Lord, after I asked you this, I thought about my husband's love. I don't always feel Don's love, but I know he loves me. When he demonstrates his love in some special way, it is a confirmation of what I already know, not evidence to establish the fact. In those times when I feel let down and disappointed by him, the greatest question is NOT, does he still love me, but rather, DO I STILL LOVE HIM?

When something goes wrong or is hurtful, I immediately accuse you of not loving me, when in reality it may be me who is questioning my love of you. Oh Lord, I see now that the question is not, do you really love me, but do I really love you? I know I want a more mature love for you. You have given me unconditional love, but I have been giving you back conditional love. I have loved you only when things go as I've expected. I love you when all makes sense or when things go well. Forgive me for returning such love to you when you have given all for me.

Perhaps you can relate. You've been waiting for what seems to be forever, and you've wondered whether God really loves you. You can't understand why he has not come through in your situation. You may even be waiting for something that you *know* is in his will, like the salvation of members of your family. You have done all you know how to do and still the situation remains unchanged. What have you missed?

Maybe nothing except the point of it all. Richard Foster wrote: "We may not see the end from the beginning, but we keep on doing what we know to do. We pray, we listen, we worship, we carry out the duty of the present moment. What we learned to do in the light of God's love, we also do in the dark of God's absence."[2]

I met Margaret at a conference in Mobile. She told me she'd been waiting her whole life to see the fruition of a promise God gave her when she was young. I asked her what she had learned from waiting. She said wisely, "I've learned to live one day at a time, to take one blessing at a time and enjoy the moment. I've learned that as I wait, I come closer to God." Another woman at the same conference slipped a small piece of paper into my hand. On it were typed these words of unknown origin:

> Special blessings are yours when God has your attention and you give God time. He wants you to move on his schedule and at his pace. He wants you to be at rest and at peace.... He wants your waiting times to be growing times.... He wants you to be still and know that he is in control. He is never late. Wait quietly, wait patiently; wait attentively. He makes all things beautiful in his time.

It's been said that the best way to learn to wait is—to wait. Yet, from the eternal perspective, waiting is not waiting at all. It is about relationship. It is about developing an intimate communion and closeness with the One who loved and gave himself in love.

A Deeper Love

When I walked down the aisle on my wedding day, I thought I could not love my husband any more than I did that day. As the door opened and I walked down the aisle, my eyes were focused on Don. I saw him standing by the altar, my handsome prince in a light gray tuxedo, smiling at me tenderly as I made my way to him. My heart was leaping with joy—this was the day I had waited for!

Had someone suggested I could love him more than I did at that moment, I would have dismissed it, because it seemed as though my heart was already filled to overflowing.

But now, as we approach seventeen years of marriage, I have come to know an even deeper love. It is not that the love I had then was not sincere, it's just that our love today is fuller. It has grown and blossomed. It has matured. This growth, however, did not come as the result of perpetual springtimes in our relationship. We have weathered the winter storms together as well, when we sometimes doubted that our relationship would survive. But now that the winter is past, we see how the roots of our marriage have grown deeper, our love has grown stronger. Our fruit tastes sweeter not in spite of winter, but *because* of it.

So it is in our relationship with God. Waiting, affliction, unanswered prayers, trials, and emotional shipwrecks are all the temporary storms that produce a deeper, more mature love for our Lord. In James 1:2 we're told to "consider it pure joy" when we face trials. I must confess I've had trouble following this. I wrote:

Thank you, Lord, for the lesson out of the book of James about trials. I see now that the interminable waiting period you have called me to is something you want me to "consider pure joy."

Lord, help me to embrace this trial of waiting as a friend you have sent my way to enrich my life. Let me welcome this "friend" as I would any other guest that I knew you had sent into my home. Allow me to enjoy the fruit which will be produced by this "friend's" visit in my life and not to shorten the visit even by one day, if it would rob me of whatever you want me to learn.

You may be in the winter of waiting. You cannot see the storm letting up any time soon. You cannot imagine how any of what you're experiencing can be a fruitful work. You miss the joy you had once known in your relationship with God. Take heart. He may have stopped the flow so as to dig deeper trenches in your life. When the springs of water burst forth again, you will have an even greater capacity for his love because you have "survived the winter."

In her book, *The Tree that Survived the Winter*, author Mary Fahy writes a dialogue between the sun and a tree which survived the winter.

"You have survived the winter because you are, and were, and always will be very much loved," said the sun. "For that small place deep within you that remained unfrozen and open to mystery, that is where I have made my dwelling. And long, long before you felt my warmth surrounding you, you were being freed and formed from within in ways so deep and profound that you could not possibly know what was happening."[3]

As I've reflected on what God has taught me, I've realized the truth of this quote. God had been working within me even before I realized it. The question is, will I remember all that I have learned in this season and apply it in the next? Did these years mature, strengthen, and establish me in God? The only way I will know is for the work to be tested and tried once more.

For some, such a never-ending process may seem discouraging. This illustration may help.

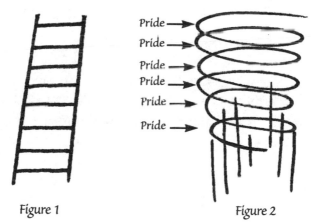

Figure 1   Figure 2

Most of us look at our spiritual journeys in a linear way (figure 1). We view our growth in terms of climbing a ladder. As we climb the ladder, we continue to move beyond the lower rungs of our issues or spiritual struggles and sometimes feel proud of our progress. Let's say rung #2 represents pride.

Once we confess and repent of that pride, we move up the spiritual ladder. But if we have climbed to rung #15 and we are convicted again of pride, what do most of us think? "Oh no!" we say. We think we've failed and feel as though we've fallen clear back to rung #2, because the issue of pride came up again.

The truth is, our spiritual journey looks more like figure 2, a spiral. Pride is on the lefthand side of the spiral. We may deal with it repeatedly, as we progressively move up and around the spiral. But notice, we are never at the same level. We may repeatedly hit issues from our past as the Holy Spirit brings us greater healing and restoration. It does not mean we failed the first time around. It only means that God is doing what he promised, to complete the work he has begun in us (Philippians 1:6) and to conform us into the image of his Son.

What most of us can't see in the midst of waiting is the deeper work that is being done in us. God wants us to enter into joyful intimacy with him. This joy is not dependent on circumstances or feelings, but is the result of resting in the presence of God.

The Joy of Intimacy

As God has tenderly wooed me into a deeper relationship with him, I have learned more about walking with him from my closest relationships than from anything else. In particular, he has used my relationship with my husband as one of his greatest teaching tools:

Lord, you promised in the book of Hosea (2:16) that I would know you as Ishi (husband) and no longer as Baali (taskmaster). I long to have such intimacy with you. I know that it all centers around trust even as it does with Don. The way he values and cherishes me abolishes the fear that he would intentionally harm me and it allows me to be vulnerable, to give myself to him freely. I am delighted to find ways to make him happy because of my love for him. I do want to know such intimacy, Lord, in my relationship with you—to love you and delight in showing you my love.

In my relationship with Don, I almost never think of "obedience." Our mutual love and openness creates such a oneness of heart that obedience is not the issue. The focus becomes communication and the uniting of our hearts.

With Don, I have discovered special ways I can bring delight and joy to his heart. Those things may vary from bringing in the trash cans on Tuesday to having a candlelight dinner in our bedroom on Friday. When I put the effort into demonstrating my love to Don in one of those special ways, I don't think about how this will make him love me more, or that I'm sure to be nominated for the Best Wife of the Year award. I simply love to bring joy to my loved one. As I do, my own joy multiplies. This is what a true love relationship is like: my joy is made complete as I seek to please the one I love.

How often I have treated my relationship with God more like a business relationship than a romance! "I'll handle this part, God.... We'll work together on this one.... You can handle this particular project, it needs a 'godly touch'....

We'll meet together weekly, and then, at the end of the month we'll print out our spreadsheet and see the results."

Because I had measured God's love by his provisions, as I interpreted them, my marriage taught me solid lessons about the truth:

Lord, forgive me for trying to find my deepest satisfaction in what you give rather than in who you are. How foolish I would be to look for the joy only in the gifts Don can give me, rather than in knowing him and resting in his love for me. I don't continually look for his next gift to me to make certain of his love, and yet I have done that with you! Let me take joy from your love alone. Help me not to depend on what is given or withheld. Please remove all of my double-mindedness.

Wellsprings of joy come from the intimacy of knowing, in the deepest part of ourselves, the love and presence of God. Nothing can rob us of that joy:

Joy is what God gives, not what we work up.... The joy that develops in the Christian way of discipleship is an overflow of spirits that comes from feeling good not about yourself but about God. We find that his ways are dependable, his promises sure. This joy is not dependent on our good luck in escaping hardship. It is not dependent on our good health and avoiding pain. Christian joy is actual in the midst of pain, suffering, loneliness, and misfortune.[4]

Run After Him

Last summer, our family traveled to Hawaii. About four or five days into the vacation, I noticed that Don and I were on very different schedules. He arose early and got in his morning walk, while the girls and I slept in. Just about the time he came back to the room, I was heading out the door to do my morning devotional, poolside. After completing my devotions and prayer time, I went back to the room as Don was coming out to get some morning sun. As I came out to join him, he was off with the girls for a morning swim in the ocean, and so forth.

The Holy Spirit said to me, "If you do not do something to help cultivate your relationship, this is what it will be like once your daughters have left home." This stopped me in my tracks. As a marriage counselor, I saw many relationships where couples had seemed to drift apart over time. Even though Don and I were not fighting or upset with each other, we were not finding ways to nurture our relationship. Without saying a word to him, I agreed to a morning ocean swim, even though I was not that excited about giving up "my" morning. Later that day, Don volunteered to accompany me shopping, which is not his most favorite activity.

Later on that evening, Don asked me to go with him down to the water's edge and watch the sunset. At first I thought, "I'd rather finish the book that I've been reading," but I'm glad I didn't. I can still picture in my mind's eye that beautifully-framed sunset, with the pinks, blues, and yellows painted across the sky. The glistening water splashed on the black volcanic rock, and the light tropical breeze blew in the palms overhead. Lying on a lounge, we embraced one another, gazing silently at the scene. Don leaned over to pick up the camera, and my body naturally leaned with him as I was enfolded in his arms. Just that moment, the Spirit of God seemed to say, "This is what I want you to experience with me—an intimacy and closeness in which there is no need to concern yourself about the direction in which I am leading. I want you to lean into me, to be so close to my heart that you will naturally follow me, as you have just done with Don."

Had I not chosen to view a sunset, I might never have known the joy of such an intimate encounter—both with my husband and with God.

For Lo, the Winter is Past

Not long ago, I spoke at a women's retreat in Alabama. My friend Allyson had organized the event and had put a lovely package of gift items together for me as a memento. She included several music cassette tapes. When I arrived home, I was busy writing and had not had much time to listen to the tapes, but I happened to grab one to take with me in the car one day. It was all Scripture which had been put to music. One particular song captivated my heart. The lyrics are based on two passages of Scripture, Jeremiah 30:17 and Song of Solomon 2:11-12 (NKJV):

For I will restore health to you and heal you of your wounds.... For lo, the winter is past, the rain is over and gone. The flowers appear on the earth; the time of singing has come....

The melody was tender, meditative. I was moved to play it several times. A few weeks later, as I was driving down the freeway listening to the tape, that song came on. Unexpectedly, the Spirit of God seemed to whisper in my heart, "Your season of waiting is over. The time of singing has come...." I felt a mixture of release, sadness, and joy as the tears slid down my cheeks. Had the harvest of joy come at last?

INEXPRESSIBLE JOY

The joy I had longed for was not the result of waiting being over. It came from a deep satisfaction of knowing God more intimately than before. G. Campbell Morgan has said it best: "Every new requirement of love is a new opportunity for my rediscovery of my Lord. Every time He confronts me and asks me to yield up something He has never asked me to yield before, there is my chance of a new vision of His face and a new unveiling of His glory...."[5]

Waiting becomes wellsprings of joy when we say "yes" to the journey. Whether he calls us to wait, to act, to step out, or to be still, our joy is in following his leading. I recorded what I felt God was trying to teach me about yielding:

> Child, I've prepared you and equipped you—now I want you to go. I am leading you in a new direction— you have not been this way before. Only follow me and learn not to rely on yourself or what you see. I will go before you and behind you. Do not fear that you will miss me, for I have prepared to take you on this journey.

It is where you will again find the peace and joy you have sought. Do not fear, my child, for I am with you. I long for you to know this. I will reveal myself to you in even greater ways as you journey with me. I will not give you the confirmation along the way as you would like, but you are to trust my power to keep you and to guide you. It is my power to lead, not your ability to follow.

Lord, what if I make a wrong turn?

I am teaching you to yield. As you yield fully to me you cannot make a mistake. It is only as you take over and try to control that you become exasperated and fearful. Yield and let go. I am calling you to a life of peaceful surrender. Do not fear, only rest in your Father's arms— I am the only place of security and rest. Come with me that your joy may be full.

Yes, waiting does become wellsprings of joy. We are no longer self-occupied, but so enraptured that we give ourselves wholly to loving and pleasing the Lover of our souls. When we love him and find joy in giving ourselves to him, an amazing thing happens. He rejoices over us and our joy is multiplied! "The Lord your God is with you, he is mighty to save. He will take great delight in you, he will quiet you with his love, he will rejoice over you with singing" (Zephaniah 3:17, NIV).

It took the waiting season to "quiet me in his love" long enough that I might enter into his joy.

Not only when thou wast born into the world did Christ love thee, but His delights were with the sons of men before there were any sons of men. Often did He think of them; from everlasting to everlasting He had set His affection upon them. What! My soul, has He been so long about thy salvation, and will not He accomplish it? Has he from everlasting been going forth to save me, and will He lose me now? What! Has He carried me in His hand, as His precious jewel, and will He now let me slip from between His fingers? Did He choose me before the mountains were brought forth, or the channels of the deep were digged, and will He reject me now? Impossible! **I am sure He would not have loved me so long if He had not been a changeless Lover. If He could grow weary of me He would have been tired of me long before now.** If He had not loved me with a love as deep as hell, and as strong as death, He would have turned from me long ago. Oh, Joy above all joys, to know that I am His everlasting and inalienable inheritance, given to Him by His Father ere the earth was! [emphasis mine][6]

As you say "yes" to waiting, may you go out in joy and be led forth in peace"! Isaiah 55:12, NIV

ELEVEN

When Waiting Becomes Worship

I could not help but worship God for his faithfulness as I heard Heather sing yesterday. I had given a short presentation for a mother-daughter tea and she sang a Twila Paris song, "A Heart that Knows You."

As I listened to the words I was moved to tears. This was my girl! Over fifteen years ago I had prayed she would have a voice to praise God with. There she was standing up in front of a hundred women and daughters offering her gift back to God. *Oh Father, how faithful you are. You heard that prayer of a young mother-to-be, who wished herself that she had a better singing voice with which to offer praise and worship to you. You heard and honored that simple prayer offered while my child was yet in the womb. There she is, Lord! Oh Father, let the words she is singing be her own heart's cry. There is no greater joy than that my child would know you and walk with you faithfully.*

Waiting becomes worship when we are able by faith to grasp a small portion of God's eternal plan. We "see" with faith eyes how his hand has worked in and through the circumstances of our lives, causing us to love him more. We worship because we can trust his love and sovereignty—he makes no mistakes concerning his children. We worship because we know him—through waiting we've drawn nearer to his heart of love.

The words of the song Heather sang have been proven in my own life:

Thought I knew so much
 But I've got so much to learn
Got so far to go
So much left to burn
Thought I knew You well
But I struggle in Your hands
Here again You bring the truth before me
Freedom only comes when I let go
This I know

(Chorus)
…And a heart that knows You
Is a heart that can wait
Die to the dearest desire
 …And a heart that knows You
Is a heart that can still celebrate
Following love through the fire

You would never lead
Where You had not been
Every road I face
You go down again
Time has come and gone
Since You walked into the flame
Still there is the pain before the glory

And it is Your will I must embrace
Oh for grace...
(Repeat Chorus)

It may be for my sake
Just to help me grow
Maybe for Your Kingdom, Lord
I don't need to know
(Repeat Chorus)[1]

"... Freedom only comes when I let go...." As I listened, I felt both joy and sorrow. Joy for the harvest I saw in Heather's life. Sorrow for the many times I had misrepresented the love of God to my child. Joy that a prayer had been answered. Sorrow that I could not protect her from the hurt of this world. Joy that she was maturing, becoming a young woman. Sorrow that in becoming a young woman, the day was approaching, all too quickly, when I would have to let her go.

Once again I was reminded of the importance of having an eternal perspective and focus. My faith, hope, and belief do not rest in what I have or haven't done to prepare my child, but my hope is in God, who promises that all who wait on him will not be ashamed (Psalms 25:3).

Many times when all is chaotic around me, when life is hard-hitting and there seems to be no rest in sight, I seek the safety and comfort of my husband's arms. Just being in his presence is comforting. As he wraps his strong arms around me and assures me with tender words like, "It's all going to work out," I can rest even while nothing changes.

Waiting becomes worship when we can do the same with God. We can hope in what we do not see because we are resting in his arms, confident that he "works all things after the counsel of his will" (Ephesians 1:11b, NASB).

"Waiting means hoping: not taking up a vaguely hopeful optimistic approach to life, but looking expectantly for specific events which there is reason for believing will materialize. 'Those who wait for Yahweh shall renew their strength' (Isaiah 40:31) means that those who are looking expectantly for the act of God which is round the corner will find that this hope gives them new strength now."[2]

Waiting in Hope

As I have searched the Scriptures in my study on what it means to wait expectantly, I discovered that the word "wait" in Hebrew is pronounced "kaw-vaw" and is used in such familiar Scriptures as: Psalms 27:14(NIV), "Wait for the Lord; be strong and take heart and wait for the Lord"; Psalms 40:1(NIV), "I waited patiently for the Lord...."; Psalms 130:5 (NIV), "I wait for the Lord, my soul waits, and in his word I put my hope"; Isaiah 40:31(NASB), "Yet those who wait for the Lord will gain new strength...."; Lamentations 3:25 (NASB), "The Lord is good to those who wait for him...."

Moreover, the word *hope* is often used interchangeably with *wait* in many of the scriptures cited above. I spoke with Dr. Ed Curtis, Hebrew professor at Biola University, who confirmed this connection between waiting and hope. He said the word hope, pronounced "tik-vaw," was derived from the Hebrew word for wait. He said "waiting" in these Scriptures implies an expectation of fulfillment—in other words, hope. It is not an empty hope or wishful thinking, it is "waiting for something you have every reason to believe will occur."[3]

Eugene Peterson further describes this expectant hope: "Hoping is not dreaming. It is not spinning an illusion of fantasy to protect us from our boredom or pain. It means a confident alert expectation that God will do what he said he will do. It is imagination put in the harness of faith. It is a willingness to let him do it his way and in his time. It is the opposite of making plans that we demand that God put into effect, telling him both how and when to do it."[4]

When we wait for God in hope, we wait with watchful expectation. The literal meaning of the Hebrew word "wait" means "to bind together, perhaps by twisting, to collect, to expect, patiently, tarry, wait (for, on or upon)."[5] As I reflected on the Hebrew words I wondered why God would choose to use such words. Why do the words imply a "twisting"?

I visualized braiding my daughters' hair. Uniformity comes with braiding as the loose strands are brought into a single beautiful form. When something is braided together it has more strength than if it were separate strands just bunched together. The picture was becoming clearer.

As we wait for God we are being braided and interwoven into relationship with him, conformed to his image and strengthened by his grace which is ever at work in us. We are being united as one, even as Jesus prayed that we might be:

"I have given them the glory that you gave me, that they may be one as we are one; I in them and you in me. May they be brought to complete unity to let the world know that you sent me and have loved them even as you have loved me."   JOHN 17:22-23 (NIV)

Waiting in hope means that we rest our faith and expectation, not in what God will do for us, but on God who *is* our hope and expectation: "But as for me, I watch in hope for the Lord, I wait for God my Savior; my God will hear me" (Micah 7:7, NIV).

Ben Patterson wrote: "To hear God's promise and call is to hear something that perhaps no one else around us can hear. It is to feel ourselves begin to tap our toes and move gently to the beat of the music, perhaps to the bewilderment of those watching us. The music we hear is the music of God's future. Hope is hearing the tune; faith is to dance to it now."[6]

Perhaps you are beginning to hear a distant melody. You can dance, you know, even if your season of waiting is not quite over with. "If we can start praising God even in trouble, and not just when it is past, then we will find that trouble itself is transformed—or rather we are transformed in it."[7] Our highest praise to God comes when we offer adoration and worship to him in the very midst of our pain, confusion, and doubt.

Waiting becomes worship when our as-yet-unfulfilled hopes and dreams take a secondary place to knowing, loving, and trusting our God. Worship wells up when we can *glance* at the temporal and *gaze* upon the eternal. "So we fix our eyes not on what is seen, but on what is unseen. For what is seen is temporary, but what is unseen is eternal" (2 Corinthians 4:18, NIV).

Waiting also brings worship as we keep an eternal perspective and focus on the harvest that God is bringing about through the waiting season.

Reaping the Harvest

Several weeks ago, Kellie proudly brought home a huge head of iceberg lettuce, the first harvest of her garden. I could hardly believe my own eyes. She really grew this! She was so thrilled as we washed it together and prepared our family's dinner salad. We were using *her* lettuce. It was truly the best lettuce I'd tasted in years. We all commented how wonderful it was and how proud we were of her efforts. As her mother, I was blessed as I saw the joy it brought my child to have contributed to the family by offering back to us the fruit of her labor.

As I thought about our celebration, I wondered if this is what it must be like for our Heavenly Father. I provided the resources for Kellie's garden, just as our Father provides the raw materials for our life's garden. I took great delight as I watched Kellie diligently attend to all that was needed to produce a harvest, and so our God delights in us as we do the hard work of cultivating the "life-plot" he has given us. At times she needed my help because I was stronger and could assist her in uprooting some stubborn weeds that were deeply embedded in the soil. So it is with God. I needed this waiting season to expose some of the weeds that had embedded themselves in my heart, and God was there helping me to root those out.

As the weeks went by, and Kellie saw the fruit of her labor springing up, here she was, willing to offer it back to the family. I was overjoyed as I saw her great pleasure in all of this. Likewise, our Father in heaven is blessed when he sees his children reaping a harvest in their lives and being willing to offer it in humility and service to others.

Mature Wheat

My friend Alma told me a true story that happened recently. Her daughter Shera was approaching her seventh birthday. Alma said for a solid month before her birthday, her daughter was asking her if she was going to be grown up now that she was about to turn seven. Each time, Alma reassured her, saying, "Yes, honey, you're growing up." She didn't realize what was going on until the morning of her daughter's birthday. Her daughter came into her bedroom crying. Alma asked, "Shera, honey, what's wrong? It's your birthday today!" Shera said through tears, "I know, Mommy, that's why I'm crying. You said I'd be grown up now that I'm seven, and I looked in the mirror and I'm just the same as I was!"

Some of you may feel this way as it relates to waiting. You may have picked up this book thinking it was going to answer all your questions and transform you from a whiner to a "godly waiter" through its pages. Instead of a quick fix, I've shared how a waiting season can be compared to the harvesting, threshing, and winnowing of grain. As we actively wait, we are allowing the Spirit of God to winnow additional impurities from our hearts and lives, the chaff that has no life-giving properties.

Finally, we come to waiting upon God where our focus is on the eternal. Waiting then becomes wisdom, wellsprings of joy and worship for our God who is ever faithful to produce a plentiful harvest in and through our lives.

We read in the letter to the Hebrews, "No discipline [such as waiting] seems pleasant at the time, but painful. Later on, however, it produces a harvest of righteousness and peace for those who have been trained by it" (Hebrews 12:11, NIV).

Harvest time is always a time of celebration. Pentecost, also known as the Feast of Weeks, was the time when the Jewish people celebrated the wheat harvest in Israel.[8] The long process is over and it is time for thanksgiving. All the tilling and planting, tending and waiting, even the work of the harvest itself, the threshing and the winnowing—are over! God's grace has produced a bountiful harvest.

Abounding Grace

As I have written these pages, I've felt that I was walking along with you, dear reader. I have been traveling the same road, perhaps only one or two steps ahead, but ever aware of my own need for the grace of my God.

I still would rather travel the known way as opposed to the unknown way, but I'm learning to listen for the music with my dancing shoes on. I know I will again go through the stages of waiting I've shared with you, but I hope as I travel, I will be more in tune with the sovereign melody of my Master composer.

I'm learning to rest in him, surrender earlier, and view waiting from an eternal perspective. I have learned to look at time differently as well. God spoke to my heart about this when I was lamenting my lack of spiritual maturity on my thirtieth spiritual birthday:

Jan, you are my daughter, in whom I am well-pleased. Your eyes are limited in perspective as you view time. Thirty years is but a vapor to me. I do not see as you see. I am working my purpose in your life. You are not too slow; you are on my timetable. I desire to give you overflowing joy that will spring forth as naturally as a fresh spring. You are in a winter now, and much seems barren and lifeless, but as the spring comes, and the melting snow brings refreshment and life to many, you will see the fruit. Remember, your part is not to make it happen—only to allow the spring to come as naturally as it follows winter. Keep your eyes on me and learn to delight in my delight over you.

I could not have imagined all the grace God had waiting for me in this process. Had I known, I never would have resisted it so! He has brought forth a harvest beyond my expectations! It is his delight to do so.

Early one morning, I wrote this:

Waiting Had a Purpose

I can finally call him Father,
I can look into his face.
The former fear that gripped my soul
is gone without a trace.

I can rest in him and find the joy
he's longed for me to hold.
It's only been through waiting
That his plans he could unfold.

I wandered and I wallowed,
I wept from deep inside.
The waiting had a purpose, Lord,
It taught me to abide.

I wondered and I wrestled,
I whined before I knew.
The waiting had a purpose, Lord,
It brought me home to you.

At home with you, a peaceful place,
To abandon is so sweet.
My one and only longing
is the day that we shall meet.
To see your face, my precious Lord,
To worship at your feet,
The day is not far off,
When my joy will be complete.

I can finally call you Daddy—
As I've longed for years to do.
The waiting had a purpose, Lord,
The purpose was in you.

There is a great mystery in all of our waitings. "Through them all it is really God who is doing all the waiting! We think we are the ones waiting for him, but in reality it is he who waits for us."[9]

God waits longingly for you, and is "able to make all grace abound to you, so that in all things at all times, having all that you need, you will abound in every good work" (2 Corinthians 9:8, NIV).

His grace abounds—especially in the waiting season.

A week after I told God that I entrusted Kellie to his care, I received a note from the teacher I had requested for her. It said, "Someone has been praying." A few days later, I was told that Kellie would be moving the following Monday to the class we had so much wanted. Later, I learned that in over twenty-five years of teaching, this beloved teacher had never before had a parent request that a child be removed from her class. However, that week a mother had requested her son be moved to the other class in order to be with his best friend, so the exchange was arranged.

Later that year, I saw Kellie's teacher in the grocery store. I told her a little about what God had done in my heart through the experience. She smiled sweetly and said, "Jan, you think God answered that prayer for you, but the truth is he answered it for me. Kellie has been a bright spot in my year! She has been a joy to have in my class." Isn't God's economy wonderful?

He is our Abba Father, "the God of all grace, who called you to his eternal glory in Christ, [who,] after you have suffered a little while, will himself restore you and make you strong, firm and steadfast. To him be the power for ever and ever. Amen" (1 Peter 5:10, NIV).

NOTES

TWO

When Waiting Brings Wondering

1. J.A.Thompson, *Handbook of Life in Bible Times* (Downer's Grove, Ill.: InterVarsity Press, 1986), 129-33.
2. James Freeman, *Manners and Customs of the Bible* (Plainfield, N.J.: Logos, 1972), 59, 129, 264-65.
3. J. A. Thompson, 131.
4. Oswald Chambers, *My Utmost for His Highest* (Westwood, N.J.: Barbour, 1963), 285.
5. Ronald Dunn, *When Heaven Is Silent* (Nashville: Nelson, 1994), 65.
6. Ben Patterson, *Waiting: Finding Hope When God Seems Silent* (Downer's Grove, Ill. : InterVarsity Press, 1989), 12.

THREE

When Waiting Brings Wandering

1. Charles H. Spurgeon, *Morning and Evening* (Peabody, Mass.: Hendrickson, 1991), 412.
2. *Leadership Journal,* Summer 1986, 59, as quoted in Patterson, Introduction.

FOUR

When Waiting Brings Whining

1. G. Campbell Morgan, *The Westminster Pulpit* (New York: Fleming H. Revell, 1954), Vol. I, 95.
2. Spurgeon, 94.
3. W.E. Vine, *Vine's Expository Dictionary of New Testament Words* (McLean, Va.: McDonald, 1987), 664.
4. Jean Shaw, *Devotions for Gardeners* (Grand Rapids, Mich.: Zondervan, 1994), 11.

FIVE

When Waiting Brings Wallowing

1. Phillip Keller, *A Shepherd Looks at Psalm 23* (Grand Rapids, Mich.: Zondervan, 1970), 60-61.
2. Harry Verploegh, *Signposts: A Collection of Sayings from A.W. Tozer* (Wheaton, Ill.: Victor, 1988), 44.
3. *Webster's Seventh New Collegiate Dictionary* (Springfield, Mass.: G. & C. Merriam, 1969), 169.
4. Eugene Peterson, *A Long Obedience in the Same Direction* (Downer's Grove, Ill.: InterVarsity Press, 1980), 139.
5. Chambers, 210.
6. David Seamands, *Healing of Memories* (Wheaton, Ill.: Victor, 1985), 95, 96.

SIX

When Waiting Brings Wrestling

1. *Webster's Seventh New Collegiate Dictionary*, 1032.

2. Richard Foster, *Prayer* (San Francisco: HarperSanFrancisco, 1992), 53.

3. Peterson, 70.

4. Patterson, 80.

5. Patterson, 142.

SEVEN

When Waiting Brings Weeping

1. Peterson, 95-96.

2. Catherine Thompson and Barbara Moore, "Grief Is Not a Sign of Weakness," *USA TODAY*, July 1991, 92-93.

3. James A. Strong, *Strong's Exhaustive Concordance*, (Gordensville, Tenn.: Dugan, n.d.), Greek dictionary, reference No.1145, 21.

4. Strong, Greek dictionary, reference 2799, 42.

5. Strong, Hebrew Dictionary, references 6937, 6939, 102.

6. Warren W. Wiersbe, *With the Word: A Devotional Commentary* (Nashville: Oliver Nelson, Division of Thomas Nelson, 1991), 344.

7. Gary Oliver, *Real Men Have Feelings Too* (Chicago: Moody, 1993), 237.

8. Mike DiGiovanna, "Ordeal Helps Carew Open Up," *Los Angeles Times*— Orange County Section, C-1, C-3.

9. Carsten Thiede, *Simon Peter: From Galilee to Rome* (Grand Rapids, Mich.: Academie Books, Zondervan, 1988), 86.

EIGHT

When Waiting Brings Willingness

1. David Runcorn, *A Center Of Quiet: Hearing God When Life Is Noisy* (Downer's Grove, Ill.: InterVarsity Press, 1990), 78.

2. Peterson, 127.

3. Chambers, 305.

4. Runcorn, 80.

5. Jack Taylor, *After the Spirit Comes* (Nashville: Broadman, 1974), 56.

6. Jack Hayford, *Rebuilding the Real You* (Ventura, Calif.: Regal, 1986), 81, 27.

7. Charles Stanley, *How to Listen to God* (Nashville: Nelson, 1985), 41.

8. A.W. Tozer, *Pursuit of God* (Camp Hill, Pa.: Christian, 1982), 28.

9. Harry Verploegh, *Signposts: A Collection of Sayings from A.W. Tozer* (Wheaton, Ill.: Victor, 1988), 161.

NINE

When Waiting Becomes Wisdom

1. Carole Mayhall, *Lord, Teach Me Wisdom* (Colorado Springs: NavPress, 1979), 18.

2. Chambers, 256.

3. Spurgeon, 50.

4. Runcorn, 88.

TEN

When Waiting Becomes Wellsprings

1. Runcorn, 80-81.

2. Foster, 23.

3. Mary Fahy, *The Tree that Survived the Winter* (New York: Paulist, 1989), 35.

4. Peterson, 96-97.

5. Morgan, Vol. I, 227.

6. Spurgeon, 117.

ELEVEN

When Waiting Becomes Worship

1. Twila Paris, "A Heart That Knows You," Ariose Music, 1992. Used by permission.

2. John Goldingay, *Songs from a Strange Land: Psalms 42-51* (Downer's Grove, Ill.: InterVarsity Press,1978), 42.

3. Goldingay, 42.

4. Peterson, 140.

5. Strong, Hebrew Dictionary, No. 6960, 102.

6. Patterson, 73.

7. Goldingay, 43.

8. Thompson, 131.

9. Patterson, 111.